The

Doctrine

of

Sanctification

A. W. Pink

The Doctrine of Sanctification

A. W. Pink

CHRISTIAN HERITAGE

Arthur W. Pink was born in Nottingham, England in 1886. He ministered in the USA, Australia and England before settling in Stornoway, Scotland where he died in 1952. For many years Pink edited a monthly magazine called *Studies in the Scriptures*, and it is from that magazine that many of Pink's publications have come.

In addition to the *Doctrine of Sanctification*, Christian Focus publishes two other titles by Pink: *The Seven Sayings of the Saviour on the Cross*(see page 223 for details) and *The Life of Faith* (see page 221)

© Christian Focus Publications

ISBN 1-85792-414-2
ISBN 978-185792-414-5

10 9 8 7 6 5 4 3 2 1

This edition published in 1998,
reprinted 2006
in the Christian Heritage Imprint
by
Christian Focus Publications, Ltd.,
Geanies House, Fearn, Ross-shire,
IV20 1TW, Great Britain.

www.christianfocus.com

Cover design by Danie Van Straaten

Printed by
J. H. Haynes, Sparkford

Contents

1

Introduction

In the articles upon 'The Doctrine of Justification' we contemplated the transcendent grace of God which provided for his people a Surety, who kept for them perfectly his holy law, and who also endured the curse which was due to their manifold transgressions against it. In consequence thereof, though in ourselves we are criminals who deserve to be brought to the bar of God's justice and there be sentenced to death, we are, nevertheless, by virtue of the accepted service of our Substitute, not only not condemned, but 'justified', that is, *pronounced righteous* in the high courts of heaven. Mercy has rejoiced against judgment: yet not without the governmental righteousness of God, as expressed in his holy law, having been fully glorified. The Son of God incarnate, as the federal head and representative of his people, obeyed it, and also suffered and died under its condemning sentence. The claims of God have been fully met, justice has been magnified, the law has been made more honourable than if every descendant of Adam had personally fulfilled its requirements.

'As respects justifying righteousness, therefore, believers have nothing to do with the law. They are justified "apart from it" (Rom. 3:21), that is, apart from any personal fulfilment thereof.

We could neither fulfil its righteousness, nor bear its course. The claims of the law were met and ended, once and forever, by the satisfaction of our great Substitute, and as a result we have attained to righteousness without works, i.e., without personal obedience of our own. "By the obedience of *one* shall many be constituted righteous' (Rom. 5:19). There may indeed, and there are, other relations in which we stand to the law. It is the principle of our *new* nature to rejoice in its holiness: "we delight in the law of God after the inner man." We know the comprehensiveness and the blessedness of those first two commandments on which all the Law and the Prophets hang: we know that "love is the fulfilling of the law". We do not despise the guiding light of the holy and immutable commandments of God, lovingly embodied, as they have been, in the ways and character of Jesus; but we do not seek to obey them with any thought of obtaining justification thereby.

'That which *has been* attained, cannot remain to be attained. Nor do we place so great an indignity on "the righteousness of our God and Saviour", as to put the partial and imperfect obedience which we render *after* we are justified, on a level with that heavenly and perfect righteousness by which we *have been* justified. *After* we have been justified, grace may and does for Christ's sake, accept as well-pleasing our imperfect obedience; but this being a consequence of our perfected justification cannot be made a ground thereof. Nor can anything that is in the least degree imperfect, be presented to God with the view of attaining justification. In respect of this, the courts of God admit of nothing that falls short of his own absolute perfectness' (B. W. Newton).

Having, then, dwelt at some length on the basic and blessed truth of justification, it is fitting that we should now consider the closely connected and complementary doctrine of sanctification. But what is 'sanctification': is it a quality or position? Is sanctification a legal thing or an experimental? that is to say, Is it something the believer has in Christ or in himself? Is it absolute or relative? by which we mean, does it admit of degree or no? is it unchanging or progressive? Are we sanctified at the time we are justified, or is sanctification a later blessing? How is this blessing obtained? By something which is done for us, or by us, or both? How may one be assured he has been sanctified: what are the characteristics, the evidences, the fruits? How are we to distinguish between sanctification by the Father, sanctification by the Son, sanctification by the Spirit, sanctification by faith, sanctification by the Word?

Is there any difference between sanctification and holiness? If so, what? Are sanctification and purification the same thing? Does sanctification relate to the soul, or the body, or both? What position does sanctification occupy in the order of divine blessings? What is the connection between regeneration and sanctification? What is the relation between justification and sanctification? Wherein does sanctification differ from glorification? Exactly what is the place of sanctification in regard to *salvation*: does it precede or follow: or is it an integral part of it? Why is there so much diversity of opinion upon these points, scarcely any two writers treating of this subject in the same manner. Our purpose here is not simply to multiply questions but to indicate the manysidedness of our present theme, and to intimate the various avenues of approach to the study of it.

Diversive indeed have been the answers returned to the above questions. Many who were ill-qualified for such a task have undertaken to write upon this weighty and difficult theme, rushing in where wiser men feared to tread. Others have superficially examined this subject through the coloured glasses of creedal attachment. Others, without any painstaking efforts of their own, have merely echoed predecessors who they supposed gave out the truth thereon. Though the present writer has been studying this subject off and on for upwards of twenty-five years, he has felt himself to be too immature and too unspiritual to write at length thereon; and even now, it is (he trusts) with fear and trembling he essays to do so: may it please the Holy

Spirit to so guide his thoughts that he may be preserved from everything which would pervert the Truth, dishonour God, or mislead his people.

We have in our library discourses on this subject and treatises on this theme by over fifty different men, ancient and modern, ranging from hyper-Calvinists to ultra-Arminians, and a number who would not care to be listed under either. Some speak with pontifical dogmatism, others with reverent caution, a few with humble diffidence. All of them have been carefully digested by us and diligently compared on the leading points. The present writer detests sectarianism (most of all in those who are the worst affected by it, while pretending to be opposed to it), and earnestly desires to be delivered from partizanship. He seeks to be profited from the labours of all, and freely acknowledges his indebtedness to men of various creeds and schools of thought. On some aspects of *this* subject he has found the Plymouth Brethren much more helpful than the Reformers and the Puritans.

The great importance of our present theme is evidenced by the prominence which is given to it in Scripture: the words 'Holy, sanctified' etc., occurring therein hundreds of times. Its importance also appears from the high value ascribed to it: it is the supreme glory of God, of the unfallen angels, of the Church. In Exodus 15:11 we read that the Lord God is 'glorious in holiness' – that is his crowning excellency. In Matthew 25:31 mention is made of the 'holy angels', for no higher honour can be ascribed them. In Ephesians 5:26, 27, we learn that the Church's glory lieth not in pomp and outward adornment, but in holiness. Its importance further appears in that *this* is the aim in all God's dispensations. He elected his people that they should be 'holy' (Eph. 1:4); Christ died that he might 'sanctify' his people (Heb. 13:12); chastisements are sent that we might be 'partakers of God's holiness' (Heb. 12:10).

Whatever sanctification be, it is the great promise of the covenant made to Christ for his people. As Thomas Boston well said, 'Among the rest of that kind, it shines like the moon among the lesser stars – as the very chief subordinate end of the Covenant of Grace, standing therein next to the glory of God, which is the chief and ultimate end thereof. The promise of preservation, of the Spirit, of quickening the dead soul, of faith, of justification, of reconciliation, of adoption, and of the enjoyment of God as our God, do tend unto it as their common centre, and stand related to it as means to their end. They are all accomplished to sinners on design to *make them holy*.' This is abundantly clear from, 'The oath which he sware to our father Abraham: that he would grant unto us, that we, being delivered out of the hand of our enemies, might serve him without fear, in holiness and righteousness before him all the days of our life' (Luke 1:73-75). In that 'oath' or covenant, sworn to Abraham as a type of Christ (our spiritual Father: Heb. 2:13), his seed's serving the Lord in holiness is held forth as the *chief* thing sworn unto the Mediator – deliverance from their spiritual enemies being a means to that end.

The supreme excellency of sanctification is affirmed in Proverbs 8:11, 'For wisdom is better than rubies; and all the things that may be desired are not to be compared to it.' 'Everyone who has read the book of Proverbs with any attention must have observed that Solomon means by "wisdom" *holiness*, and by "folly" *sin*; by a wise man a saint, and by a fool a sinner. "The wise shall inherit glory: but shame shall be the promotion of fools" (Prov. 3:35): who can doubt whether by "the wise" he means *saints*, and by "fools" *sinners*! "The fear of the LORD is the beginning of wisdom" (Prov. 9:10), by which he means to assert that true "wisdom" is true piety or real holiness. Holiness, then, is "better than rubies", and all things that are to be desired are not to be compared with it. It is hard to conceive how

11

the inestimable worth and excellency of holiness could be painted in brighter colours than by comparing it to rubies – the richest and most beautiful objects in nature' (Nathaniel Emmons).

Not only is true sanctification an important, essential, and unspeakably precious thing, it is wholly *supernatural*.

'It is our duty to enquire into the nature of evangelical holiness, as it is a fruit or effect in us of the Spirit of sanctification, because it is abstruse and mysterious, and indiscernible unto the eye of carnal reason. We say of it in some sense as Job of wisdom, "whence cometh wisdom, and where is the place of understanding, seeing it is hid from the eyes of all living, and kept close from the fowls of heaven; destruction and death say, We have heard the fame thereof with our ears: God understandeth the way thereof, and he knoweth the place thereof. And unto man he said, Behold, the fear of the Lord that is wisdom, and to depart from evil is understanding" (28:20-23, 28). This is that wisdom whose ways, residence, and paths, are so hidden from the natural reason and understandings of men.

'No man, I say, by mere sight and conduct can know and understand aright the true nature of evangelical holiness; and it is, therefore, no wonder if the doctrine of it be despised by many as an enthusiastical fancy. It is of the things of the Spirit of God, yea, it is the principal effect of all his operation in us and towards us. And "these things of God knoweth no man but the Spirit of God" (1 Cor. 2:11). It is by him alone that we are enabled to "know the things that are freely given unto us of God" (v. 12) as this is, if ever we receive anything of him in this world, or shall do so to eternity. "Eye hath not seen, nor ear heard, neither have entered into the heart of man, the things that God hath prepared for them that love him"; the comprehension of these things is not the work of any of our natural faculties, but "God reveals them unto us by his Spirit" (vv. 9, 10).

'Believers themselves are oft-times much unacquainted with it, either as to their apprehensions of its true nature, causes, and effects, or, at least, as to their own interests and concernment therein. As we know not of ourselves, the things that are wrought in us of the Spirit of God, so we seldom attend as we ought unto his instruction of us in them. It may

seem strange indeed, that, whereas all believers are sanctified
and made holy, they should not understand nor apprehend
what is wrought in them and for them, and what abideth
with them: but, alas, how little do we know of ourselves, of
what we are, and whence are our powers and faculties even
in things natural. Do we know how the members of the body
are fashioned in the womb?' (John Owen)

Clear proof that true sanctification is wholly supernatural
and altogether beyond the ken of the unregenerate, is
found in the fact that so many are thoroughly deceived and
fatally deluded by fleshly imitations and Satanic substitutes
of real holiness. It would be outside our present scope to
describe in detail the various pretentions which pose as
gospel holiness, but the poor Papists, taught to look up to
the 'saints' canonized by their 'church', are by no means
the only ones who are misled in this vital matter. Were it
not that God's Word reveals so clearly the power of that
darkness which rests on the understanding of all who are
not taught by the Spirit, it would be surprising beyond
words to see so many intelligent people supposing that
holiness consists in abstinence from human comforts,
garbing themselves in mean attire, and practising various
austerities which God has never commanded.

Spiritual sanctification can only be rightly apprehended
from what God has been pleased to reveal thereon in his
holy Word, and can only be experimentally known by the
gracious operations of the Holy Spirit. We can arrive at no
accurate conceptions of this blessed subject except as our
thoughts are formed by the teaching of Scripture, and we
can only experience the power of the same as the Inspirer of
those Scriptures is pleased to write them upon our hearts.
Nor can we obtain so much as a correct idea of the meaning
of the term 'sanctification' by limiting our attention to a few
verses in which the word is found, or even to a whole class
of passages of a similar nature: there must be a painstaking

examination of *every* occurrence of the term and also of its cognates; only thus shall we be preserved from the entertaining of a one-sided, inadequate, and misleading view of its fullness and many-sidedness.

Even a superficial examination of the Scriptures will reveal that holiness is *the opposite of sin*, yet the realization of this at once conducts us into the realm of mystery, for how can persons be sinful and holy at one and the same time? It is *this* difficulty which so deeply exercises the true saints: they perceive in themselves so much carnality, filth, and vileness, that they find it almost impossible to believe that *they* are HOLY. Nor is the difficulty solved here, as it was in justification, by saying, Though we are completely unholy in ourselves, we *are* holy *in Christ*. We must not here anticipate the ground which we hope to cover, except to say, the Word of God clearly teaches that those who have been sanctified by God *are* holy *in themselves*. The Lord graciously prepare our hearts for what is to follow.

2
Its Meaning

Having dwelt at some length upon the relative or legal change which takes place in the *status* of God's people at justification, it is fitting that we should now proceed to consider the real and experimental change that takes place in their *state*, which change is begun at their sanctification and made perfect in glory. Though the justification and the sanctification of the believing sinner may be, and should be, contemplated singly and distinctively, yet they are inseparably connected, God never bestowing the one without the other; in fact we have no way or means whatsoever of knowing the former apart from the latter. In seeking to arrive at the meaning of the second, it will therefore be of help to examine its relation to the first. 'These individual companies, sanctification and justification, must not be disjoined: under the law the ablutions and oblations went together, the washings and the sacrifices' (Thomas Manton).

There are two principal effects that sin produces, which cannot be separated: the filthy defilement it causes, the awful guilt it entails. Thus, salvation from sin necessarily requires both a cleansing and a clearing of the one who is to be saved. Again; there are two things absolutely indispensable in order for any creature to dwell with God

15

in heaven: a valid title to that inheritance, a personal fitness to enjoy such blessedness – the one is given in justification, the other is commenced in sanctification. The inseparability of the two things is brought out in, 'In the LORD have I righteousness and strength' (Isa. 45:24); 'but of him are ye in Christ Jesus, who of God is made unto us wisdom, and righteousness, and sanctification, and redemption' (1 Cor. 1:30); 'but ye are washed, but ye are sanctified, but ye are justified' (1 Cor. 6:11); 'If we confess our sins, he is faithful and just to forgive us our sins, *and to cleanse* us from all unrighteousness' (1 John 1:9).

> 'These blessings walk hand in hand; and never were, never will be, never can be parted. No more than the delicious scent can be separated from the beautiful bloom of the rose or carnation: let the flower be expanded, and the fragrance transpires. Try if you can separate gravity from the stone or heat from the fire. If these bodies and their essential properties, if these causes and their necessary effects, are indissolubly connected, so are our justification and our sanctification' (James Hervey).
>
> 'Like as Adam alone did personally break the first covenant by the all-ruining offence, yet they to whom his guilt is imputed, do thereupon become inherently sinful, through the corruption of nature conveyed to them from him; so Christ alone did perform the condition of the second covenant, and those to whom his righteousness is imputed, do thereupon become inherently righteous, through inherent grace communicated to them from him by the Spirit. "For if by one man's offence death reigned by one, much more they which receive the abundance of grace and of the gift of righteousness, shall reign in life by one, Jesus Christ" (Rom. 5:17). How did death reign by Adam's offence? Not only in point of guilt, whereby his posterity were bound over to destruction, but also in point of their being dead to all good, dead in trespasses and sins. Therefore the receivers of the gift of righteousness must thereby be brought to reign in life, not only legally in justification, but also morally in sanctification' (Thomas Boston).

Though absolutely inseparable, yet these two great blessings of divine grace are quite distinct. In sanctification something is actually *imparted* to us, in justification it is only *imputed*. Justification is based entirely upon the work Christ wrought *for* us, sanctification is principally a work wrought *in* us. Justification respects its object in a legal sense and terminates in a relative change – a deliverance from punishment, a right to the reward; sanctification regards its object in a moral sense, and terminates in an experimental change both in character and conduct – imparting a love for God, a capacity to worship him acceptably, and a meetness for heaven. Justification is by a righteousness without us, sanctification is by a holiness wrought in us. Justification is by Christ as Priest, and has regard to the penalty of sin; sanctification is by Christ as King, and has regard to the dominion of sin: the former cancels its damning power, the latter delivers from its reigning power.

They differ, then, in their *order* (not of time, but in their nature), justification preceding, sanctification following: the sinner is pardoned and restored to God's favour before the Spirit is given to renew him after his image. They differ in their *design:* justification removes the obligation unto punishment; sanctification cleanses from pollution. They differ in their *form:* justification is a judicial act, by which the sinner is pronounced righteous; sanctification is a moral work, by which the sinner is made holy: the one has to do solely with our standing before God, the other chiefly concerns our state. They differ in their *cause:* the one issuing from the merits of Christ's satisfaction, the other proceeding from the efficacy of the same. They differ in their *end:* the one bestowing a title to everlasting glory, the other being the highway which conducts us thither. 'And an highway shall be there, ... and it shall be called The way of holiness' (Isa. 35:8).

The words 'holiness' and 'sanctification' are used in our English Bible to represent one and the same word in the Hebrew and Greek originals, but they are by no means used with a uniform signification, being employed with quite a varied latitude and scope. Hence it is hardly to be wondered at that theologians have framed so many different definitions of its meaning. Among them we may cite the following, each of which, save the last, having an element of truth in them. 'Sanctification is Godlikeness, or being renewed after his image.' 'Holiness is conformity to the law of God, in heart and life. Sanctification is a freedom from the tyranny of sin, into the liberty of righteousness.' 'Sanctification is that work of the Spirit whereby we are fitted to be worshippers of God.' 'Holiness is a process of cleansing from the pollution of sin.' 'It is a moral renovation of our natures whereby they are made more and more like Christ.' 'Sanctification is the total eradication of the carnal nature, so that sinless perfection is attained in this life.'

Another class of writers, held in high repute in certain circles, and whose works now have a wide circulation, have formed a faulty, or at least very inadequate, definition of the word 'sanctify', through limiting themselves to a certain class of passages where the term occurs and making deductions from only one set of facts. For example: not a few have cited verse after verse in the Old Testament. where the world 'holy' is applied to inanimate objects, like the vessels of the tabernacle, and then have argued that the term itself cannot possess a *moral* value. But that is false reasoning: it would be like saying that because we read of the 'everlasting hills' (Gen. 49:26) and the 'everlasting mountains' (Hab. 3:6) that therefore *God* cannot be 'everlasting' – which is the line of logic (?) employed by many of the Universalists so as to set aside the truth of the everlasting punishment of the wicked.

Words *must* first be used of *material* objects before we are ready to employ them in a higher and abstract sense. All our ideas are admitted through the medium of the physical senses, and consequently refer in the first place to external objects; but as the intellect develops we apply those names, given to material things, unto those which are immaterial. In the earliest stages of human history, God dealt with his people according to this principle. It is true that God's sanctifying of the Sabbath day teaches us that the first meaning of the word is 'to set apart', but to argue from this that the term never has a moral force when it is applied to moral agents is not worthy of being called 'reasoning' – it is a mere begging of the question: as well argue that since in a majority of passages 'baptism' has reference to the immersion of a person in water, it can never have a mystical or spiritual force and value – which is contradicted by Luke 12:50 and 1 Corinthians 12:13.

The outward ceremonies prescribed by God to the Hebrews with regard to their external form of religious service were all designed to teach corresponding inward duties, and to show the obligation unto moral virtues. But so determined are many of our moderns to empty the word 'sanctify' of all moral value, they quote such verses as 'for their sakes I sanctify myself' (John 17:19); and inasmuch as there was no sin in the Lord Jesus from which he needed cleansing, have triumphantly concluded that the thought of moral purification *cannot* enter into the meaning of the word when it is applied to his people. This also is a serious error – what the lawyers would call 'special pleading': with just as much reason might we insist that the word 'tempt' can never signify to solicit and incline to evil, because it cannot mean *that* when used of Christ in Matthew 4:1 and Hebrews 4:15!

The only satisfactory way of ascertaining the meaning or meanings of the word 'sanctify' is to carefully examine every passage in which it is found in Holy Writ, studying its setting, weighing any term with which it is contrasted, observing the objects or persons to which it is applied. This calls for much patience and care, yet only thus do we obey

19

THE DOCTRINE OF SANCTIFICATION

that exhortation 'prove all things' (1 Thess. 5:21). That this term denotes more than simply 'to separate' or 'set apart', is clear from Numbers 6:8 where it is said of the Nazarite, 'all the days of his separation he is *holy* unto the Lord', for according to some that would merely signify 'all the days of his separation he is *separated* unto the Lord', which would be meaningless tautology. So again, of the Lord Jesus we are told, that he was '*holy*, harmless, undefiled, *separate from sinners*' (Heb. 7:26), which shows that 'holy' means something more than 'separation'.

That the word 'sanctify' (or 'holy' – the *same* Hebrew or Greek term) is far from being used in a uniform sense is clear from the following passages. In Isaiah 66:17 it is said of certain wicked men, 'They that sanctify themselves, and purify themselves in the gardens behind one tree in the midst, eating swine's flesh.' In Isaiah 13:3 God said of the Medes, whom he had appointed to overthrow the Babylonian empire: 'I have commanded my sanctified ones, I have also called my mighty ones, for mine anger.' When applied to God himself, the term denotes his ineffable majesty, 'Thus saith the high and lofty One that inhabiteth eternity, whose name is Holy' (Isa. 57:15 and cf. Ps. 99:3; Hab. 3:3). It also includes the thought of adorning and equipping: 'thou shalt anoint it, to sanctify it' (Exod. 29:36 and cf. 40:11); 'anointed him, to sanctify him' (Lev. 8:12 and cf. v. 30), 'If a man therefore purge himself from these, he shall be a vessel unto honour, sanctified *and meet for the Master's use*' (2 Tim. 2:21).

That the word 'holy' or 'sanctify' has in many passages a reference to a *moral quality* is clear from such verses as the following: 'Wherefore the law is holy, and the commandment holy, and just, and good' (Rom. 7:12) – each of those predicates are moral qualities. Among the identifying marks of a scriptural bishop are that he must be 'a lover of hospitality, a lover of good men, sober, just, holy, temperate' (Titus 1:8) – each of those are moral qualities, and the very connection in which the term 'holy' is there found proves conclusively it means much more than an external setting apart. 'As ye have yielded your members servants to uncleanness and to iniquity, even so now yield your members servants to righteousness unto holiness' (Rom. 6:19): here the word 'holiness' is used antithetically to 'uncleanness'. So again in 1 Corinthians 7:14, 'else were your children *unclean*; but now are they *holy*' i.e. maritally pure.

That sanctification includes *cleansing* is clear from many considerations. It may be seen in the types, 'Go unto the people, and *sanctify* them today and tomorrow, and let them *wash* their clothes' (Exod. 19:10) – the latter being an emblem of the former. As we have seen in Romans 6:19 and 1 Corinthians 7:14, it is *the opposite* of 'uncleanness'. So also in 2 Timothy 2:21 the servant of God is to *purge* himself from 'the vessels of dishonour' (worldly, fleshy, and apostate preachers and churches) if he is to be 'sanctified' and 'meet for the Master's use'. In Ephesians 5:26 we are told that Christ gave himself for the Church, 'that he might *sanctify and cleanse it*', and that, in order that he 'might present it to himself a glorious Church, not having spot or wrinkle or any such thing, but (in contrast from such blemishes) that it should be *holy*' (v. 27). 'If the blood of bulls and goats, and the ashes of a heifer sprinkling the unclean, sanctifieth to the purifying of the flesh' (Heb. 9:13): what could be plainer! – ceremonial sanctification under the law was secured by a process of *purification or cleansing*.

> 'Purification is the first proper notion of internal real sanctification. To be unclean absolutely, and to be holy, are universally opposed. Not to be purged from sin, is an expression of an unholy person, as to be cleansed is of him that is holy. This purification is ascribed unto all the causes and means of sanctification. Not that sanctification consists wholly herein, but firstly and necessarily it is required thereunto: "I will

sprinkle clean water upon you, and ye shall be clean: from all your filthiness and from all your idols will I cleanse you!" (Ezek. 36:25). That this sprinkling of clean water upon us is the communication of the Spirit unto us for the end designed, I have before evinced. It hath also been declared wherefore he is called 'water' or compared thereunto. The next verse shows expressly that it is the Spirit of God which is intended: "I will put my Spirit within you, and cause you to walk in my statutes." And that which he is thus in the first place promised for, is the cleaning of us from the pollution of sin, which in order of nature, is proposed unto his enabling us to walk in God's statutes' (John Owen).

To sanctify, then, means in the great majority of instances, to appoint, dedicate or set apart unto God, for a holy and special use. Yet that act of separation is not a bare change of situation, so to speak, but is preceded or accompanied by a work which (ceremonially or experimentally) *fits* the person for God. Thus the priests in their sanctification (Lev. 8) were sanctified by washing in water (type of regeneration: Titus 3:5), having the blood applied to their persons (type of justification: Rom. 5:9), and being anointed with oil (type of receiving the Holy Spirit: 1 John 2:20, 27). As the term is applied to Christians it is used to designate three things, or three parts of one whole: first, the *process* of setting them apart unto God or constituting them holy: Hebrews 13:12; 2 Thessalonians 2:13; second, the *state* or condition of holy separation into which they are brought: 1 Corinthians 1:2; Ephesians 4:24; third, the personal sanctity or *holy living* which proceeds from the state: Luke 1:75; 1 Peter 1:15.

To revert again to the Old Testament types – which are generally the best interpreters of the doctrinal statements of the New Testament, providing we carefully bear in mind that the antitype is always of a higher order and superior nature to what prefigured it, as the substance must excel the shadow, the inward and spiritual surpassing the merely outward and ceremonial. 'Sanctify unto me all the firstborn

... *it is mine'* (Exod. 13:2). This comes immediately after the deliverance of the firstborn by the blood of the paschal lamb in the preceding chapter: first justification, and then sanctification as the complementary parts of one whole. 'Ye shall therefore put difference between clean beasts and unclean, and between unclean fowls and clean: and ye shall not make your souls abominable by beast, or by fowl, or by any manner of living thing that creepeth on the ground, which I have separated from you as unclean. And ye shall be holy unto me: for I the Lord am holy, and have severed you from other people, that ye should *be mine'* (Lev. 20:25, 26). Here we see there was a separation *from* all that is unclean, with an unreserved and exclusive devotement *to* the Lord.

3

Its Necessity

It is our earnest desire to write this chapter not in a theological or merely abstract way, but in a *practical* manner: in such a strain that it may please the Lord to speak through it to our needy hearts and search our torpid consciences. It is a most important branch of our subject, yet one from which we are prone to shrink, being very unpalatable to the flesh. Having been shapen in iniquity and conceived in sin (Ps. 51:5), our hearts *naturally* hate holiness, being opposed to any experimental acquaintance with the same. As the Lord Jesus told the religious leaders of his day, 'This is the condemnation, that light is come into the world, and men loved darkness rather than light' (John 3:19), which may justly be paraphrased 'men loved sin rather than holiness', for in Scripture 'darkness' is the emblem of sin – the evil one being denominated 'the power of darkness' – as 'light' is the emblem of the ineffably Holy One (1 John 1:5).

But though by nature man is opposed to the light, it is written, 'Follow peace with all men, and holiness, without which no man shall see the Lord' (Heb. 12:14). To the same effect the Lord Jesus declared 'Blessed are the pure in heart: for *they* shall see God' (Matt. 5:8). *God will not call unto nearness with himself those who are carnal and corrupt.* 'Can two walk together: except they be agreed?' (Amos 3:3): what concord can there be between an unholy soul and the thrice holy God? Our God is 'glorious in holiness' (Exod. 15:11), and therefore those whom he separates unto himself must be suited to himself, and be made 'partakers of his holiness' (Heb. 12:10). The whole of his ways with man exhibit this principle, and his Word continually proclaims that he is 'not a God that hath pleasure in wickedness: neither shall evil dwell with him' (Ps. 5:4).

By our fall in Adam we lost not only the favour of God, but also the purity of our natures, and therefore we need to be both reconciled to God and sanctified in our inner man. There is now a spiritual leprosy spread over all our nature which makes us loathsome to God and puts us into a state of separation from him. No matter what pains the sinner takes to be rid of his horrible disease, he does but hide and not cleanse it. Adam concealed neither his nakedness nor the shame of it by his fig-leaf contrivance; so those who have no other covering for their natural filthiness than the externals of religion rather proclaim than hide it. Make no mistake on this score: neither the outward profession of Christianity nor the doing of a few good works will give us access to the thrice Holy One. Unless we are washed by the Holy Spirit, and in the blood of Christ, from our native pollutions, we cannot enter the kingdom of glory.

Alas, with what *forms of godliness*, outward appearances, external embellishments are most people satisfied. How they mistake the shadows for the substance, the means for the end itself. How many devout Laodiceans are there who *know not* that they are 'wretched and miserable, and poor and blind, and naked' (Rev. 3:17). No preaching affects them, nothing will bring them to exclaim with the prophet, 'O my God, I am ashamed and blush to lift up my face to thee, my God' (Ezra 9:6). No, if they do but preserve themselves from the known guilt of such sins as are punishable among men, to all other things their conscience seems dead: they have no inward shame for anything between their souls and God, especially not for the depravity and defile-ment of their natures: of *that* they know, feel, bewail nothing.

'There is a generation that are pure in their own eyes, and yet is not washed from their filthiness' (Prov. 30:12). Although they had never been cleansed by the Holy Spirit, nor their hearts purified by faith (Acts 15:9), yet they esteemed themselves to be pure, and had not the least sense of their foul defilement. Such a generation were the self-righteous Pharisees of Christ's day: they were constantly cleansing their hands and cups, engaged in an interminable round of ceremonial washings, yet were they thoroughly ignorant of the fact that within they were filled with all manner of defilement (Matt. 23:25-28). So is a generation of churchgoers today; they are orthodox in their views, reverent in their demeanour, regular in their contributions, *but they make no conscience of the state of their hearts*.

That sanctification or personal holiness, which we here desire to show the absolute necessity of, lies in or consists of three things. First, that internal change or renovation of our souls, whereby our minds, affections and wills are brought into harmony with God. Second, that impartial compliance with the revealed will of God in all duties of obedience and abstinence from evil, issuing from a principle of faith and love. Third, that directing of all our actions unto the glory of God, by Jesus Christ, according to the gospel. This, and nothing short of this, is evangelical and saving sanctification. *The heart must be changed so as to be brought into conformity with God's nature and will*: its motives, desires, thoughts and actions require to be purified. There must be a spirit of holiness working within so as to sanctify our outward performances if they are to be acceptable unto him in whom 'there is no darkness at all'.

Evangelical holiness consists not only in external works of piety and charity, but in pure thoughts, impulses and affections of the soul, chiefly in that disinterested love from which all good works must flow if they are to receive the approbation of heaven. Not only must there be an abstinence from the execution of sinful lusts, but *there must be a loving and delighting to do the will of God in a cheerful manner*, obeying him without repining or grudging against any duty, as if it were a grievous yoke to be borne. Evangelical sanctification is that holiness of heart which causes us to love God supremely, so as to yield ourselves wholly up to his constant service in all things, and to his disposal of us as our absolute Lord, whether it be for prosperity or adversity, for life or death; and to love our neighbours as ourselves.

This entire sanctification of our whole inner and outer man is absolutely indispensable. As there must be a change of *state* before there can be of *life* – 'make the tree good, and his fruit (will be) good' (Matt. 12:33) – so there must be sanctification before there can be glorification. Unless we are purged from the pollution of sin, we can never be fit for communion with God. 'And there shall in no wise enter into it (the eternal dwelling place of God and his people) anything that defileth, neither whatsoever worketh abomination' (Rev. 21:27). 'To suppose that an unpurged sinner can be brought into the blessed enjoyment of God, is to overthrow both the law and the gospel, and to say that Christ died in vain' (J. Owen). Personal holiness is equally imperative as is the forgiveness of sins in order to eternal bliss.

Plain and convincing as should be the above statements, there is a class of professing Christians who wish to regard the justification of the believer as constituting almost the whole of his salvation, instead of its being only one aspect thereof. Such people delight to dwell upon the imputed righteousness of Christ, but they evince little or no concern about personal holiness. On the other hand, there are not a few who in their reaction from a one-sided emphasis upon justification by grace through faith alone, have gone to the opposite extreme, making sanctification the sum and substance of all their thinking and preaching. Let it be solemnly realized that while a man may learn thoroughly the scriptural doctrine of justification and yet not be *himself* justified before God, so he may be able to detect the crudities and errors of 'the Holiness people', and yet be completely unsanctified himself. But it is chiefly the first of these two errors we now desire to expose, and we cannot do better than quote at length from one who has most helpfully dealt with it.

'We are to look upon holiness as a very necessary *part of* that *salvation* that is received by faith in Christ. Some are so drenched in a covenant of works, that they accuse us for making good works needless to salvation, if we will not acknowledge them to be necessary, either as *conditions to procure* an interest in Christ, or as *preparatives to fit us* for receiving him by faith. And others, when they are taught by the Scriptures that we are saved by faith, even by faith without works, do begin to disregard all obedience to the law as not at all necessary to salvation, and do account themselves obliged to it only in point of gratitude; if it be wholly neglected, they doubt not but free grace will save them nevertheless. Yea, some are given up to such strong Antinomian delusions, that they account it a part of the liberty from bondage of the law purchased by the blood of Christ, to make no conscience of breaking the law in their conduct.

'One cause of these errors that are so contrary one to the other is that many are prone to imagine nothing else to be meant by "salvation" but to be delivered from hell, and to enjoy heavenly happiness and glory; hence they conclude that, if good works be *a means* of glorification, and precedent to it, they must also be a precedent means of our *whole* salvation, and if they be not a necessary means of our *whole* salvation, they are not at all necessary to glorification. But though "salvation" be often taken in Scripture *by way of eminency* for its perfection in the state of heavenly glory, yet, according to its full and *proper* signification, we are to understand by it all that freedom from the evil of our natural corrupt state, and all those holy and happy enjoyments that we receive from Christ our Saviour, either in this world by faith, or in the world to come by glorification. Thus, justification, the gift of the Spirit to dwell in us, the privilege of adoption (deliverance from the *reigning* power of indwelling sin, A.W.P.) are *parts* of our "salvation" which we partake of in this life. Thus also, the conformity of our hearts to the law of God, and the fruits of righteousness with which we are filled by Jesus Christ in this life, are a *necessary part of* our "salvation".

'God saveth us from our sinful uncleanness *here*, by the washing of regeneration and renewing of the Holy Spirit (Ezek. 36:29; Titus 3:5), as well as from hell hereafter. Christ was called Jesus, i.e., a Saviour: because he saves his people from their sins (Matt. 1:21). Therefore, deliverance from our sins *is part of* our "salvation", which is begun in this life by justification and sanctification, and perfected by glorification in the life to come. Can we rationally doubt whether it be any proper part of our salvation by Christ to be quickened, so as to be enabled to live to God, when we were by nature dead in trespasses and sins, and to have the image of God in holiness and righteousness restored to us, which we lost by the Fall; and to be freed from a vile dishonourable slavery to Satan and our own lusts, and made the servants of God; and to be honoured so highly as to walk by the Spirit, and bring forth the fruits of the Spirit? and what is all this but holiness in heart and life?

'Conclude we, then, that holiness in this life is *absolutely necessary to salvation*, not only as a means to the end, but by a nobler kind of necessity – as part of the end itself. Though we are saved by good works as *procuring causes*, yet we are saved to good works, as fruits and effects of saving grace, "which God hath prepared that we should walk in them" (Eph. 2:10). It is, indeed, one part of our salvation to be delivered from the bondage of the covenant of works; but the end of this is, not that we may have liberty to sin (which is the worst of slavery) but that we may fulfil the royal law of liberty, and that "we may serve in newness of spirit, and not in the oldness of the letter" (Gal. 5:13; Rom. 7:6). Yea, holiness in this life is such *a part of* our "salvation" that it is *a necessary means* to make us meet to be partakers of the inheritance of the saints in heavenly light and glory: for without holiness we can never see God (Heb. 12:14), and are as unfit for his glorious presence as swine for the presence-chamber of an earthly king.

'The last thing to be noted in this direction is that holiness of heart and life is to be sought for earnestly *by faith* as a very necessary part of our "salvation". Great multitudes of ignorant people that live under the gospel, harden their hearts in sin and ruin their souls forever, by trusting on Christ for such an *imaginary* "salvation" as consisteth not at all in *holiness*, but only in forgiveness of sin and deliverance from everlasting torments. They would be free from the *punishments* due to sin, but they love their lusts so well that they hate holiness and desire not to be saved from the *service* of sin. The way to oppose this pernicious delusion is not to deny, as some do, that trusting on Christ for salvation is a saving act of faith, but rather to show that *none do* or can trust on Christ for *true* "salvation" except they trust on him *for holiness*, neither do they heartily desire true salvation, if they do not desire to be made holy and righteous in their hearts and lives. If ever God and Christ gave you "salvation", *holiness will be one part of it*; if Christ wash you not from the filth of your sins, you have no part with him (John 13:8).

'What a strange kind of salvation do they desire that care not for holiness! They would be saved and yet be altogether dead in sin, aliens from the life of God, bereft of the image of God, deformed by the image of Satan, his slaves and vassals to their own filthy lusts, utterly unmeet for the enjoyment of God in glory. Such a salvation as that was never purchased by the blood of Christ; and those that seek it abuse the grace of God in Christ, and turn it into lasciviousness. They would be saved by Christ, and yet be *out* of Christ in a fleshly state; whereas God doth free none from condemnation but those that are in Christ, that walk not after the flesh, but after the Spirit; or else they would divide Christ, and take a part of his salvation and leave out the rest; but Christ is not divided (1 Cor. 1:13). They would have their sins forgiven, not that they may walk with God in love, in time to come, but that they may practise their enmity against him without any fear of punishment. But let them not be deceived, God is not mocked. *They understand not what true salvation is,* neither were they ever yet thoroughly sensible of their lost estate, and of the great evil of sin; and that which they trust on Christ for is but an imagin-ation of their own brains; and therefore their trusting is gross presumption.

'The gospel-faith maketh us to come to Christ with a thirsty appetite that we may drink of living water, even of his sanctifying Spirit (John 7:37, 38), and cry out earnestly to him to save us, not only from hell, but from sin, saying, "Teach us to do thy will; thy Spirit is good" (Ps. 143:10); "Turn thou me, and I shall be turned" (Jer. 31:18); "Create in me a clean heart, O God, and renew a right spirit within me" (Ps. 51:10). This is the way whereby the doctrine of salvation by grace doth necessitate us to holiness of life, by constraining us to seek for it by faith in Christ, *as a substantial part* of that "salvation" which is freely given to us through Christ' (Walter Marshall, 1692).

The above is a much longer quotation than we usually make from others, but we could not abbreviate without losing much of its force. We have given it, not only because it is one of the clearest and strongest statements we have met with, but because it will indicate that the doctrine we are advancing is no novel one of our own, but one which was much insisted upon by the Puritans. Alas, that so few today have any real scriptural apprehension of what *salvation* really is; alas that many preachers are substituting an imaginary 'salvation' which is fatally deceiving the great majority of their hearers. Make no mistake upon this point, dear reader, we beg you: if your heart is yet unsanctified, you are still unsaved; and *if you pant not after personal holiness*, then you are without any real desire for *God's* salvation.

The salvation which Christ purchased for his people includes both justification and sanctification. The Lord Jesus saves not only from the guilt and penalty of sin, but from the power and pollution of it. Where there is a genuine longing to be freed from the love of sin, there is a true desire for *his* salvation; but where there is no practical deliverance from the service of sin, then we are strangers to his saving grace. Christ came here to 'perform the mercy promised to our fathers, and to remember his holy covenant: the oath which he sware to our father Abraham; that he would grant unto us, that we being delivered out of the hand of our enemies might serve him without fear, in holiness and righteousness before him all the days of our life' (Luke 1:72-75). It is *by this* we are to test or measure ourselves: *are we* serving him 'in holiness and righteousness'? If we are not, we have not been sanctified; and if we are unsanctified, we are none of his.

Its Necessity (Completed)

In the first part of our treatment of the necessity of sanctification it was shown that, the making of a sinner holy is indispensable unto his salvation, yea, that sanctification is an integral part of salvation itself. One of the most serious defects in modern ministry is the ignoring of this basic fact. Of only too many present-day 'converts' does it have to be said, 'Ephraim is a cake not turned' (Hosea 7:8) – browned underneath, unbaked on the top. Christ is set forth as a fire-escape from hell, but not as the great Physician to deal with the malady of indwelling sin, and to fit for heaven. Much is said upon how to obtain forgiveness of sins, but little is preached on how to be cleansed from its pollutions. The necessity of his atoning blood is set forth, but not the indispensability of experimental holiness. Consequently, thousands who mentally assent to the sufficiency of Christ's sacrifice, know nothing about heart purity.

Again; there is a woeful disproportion between the place which is given to faith and the emphasis which the Scriptures give to that obedience which flows from sanctification. It is not only true that 'without faith it is impossible to please God' (Heb. 11:6), but it is equally true that without holiness 'no man shall see the Lord' (Heb. 12:14). Not only are we told 'in Christ Jesus neither circumcision availeth anything, nor uncircumcision, but a new creature' (Gal. 6:15), but it is also written, 'Circumcision is nothing, and uncircumcision is nothing, *but the keeping of the commandments of God*' (1 Cor. 7:19). It is not for nothing that God has told us, '*Godliness* is profitable unto all things, having promise of the life that now is, *and* of that which is to come' (1 Tim. 4:8). Not only is there in all the promises a particular respect unto personal, vital and practical 'godliness', but it is that very godliness which, pre-eminently, gives the saint an especial interest in those promises.

Alas, how many there are today who imagine that if they have 'faith', it is sure to be well with them at the end, even though they are not holy. Under the pretence of honouring faith, Satan, as an angel of light, has deceived, and is still deceiving, multitudes of souls. But when their 'faith' be examined and tested, what is it worth? Nothing at all so far as insuring an entrance into heaven is concerned: it is a powerless, lifeless, and fruitless thing; it is nothing better than that faith which the demons have (James 2:19). The faith of God's elect is unto 'the acknowledgement of the truth *which is after godliness*' (Titus 1:1). Saving faith is a 'most holy faith' (Jude 20): it is a faith which 'purifieth the heart' (Acts 15:9), it is a faith which 'worketh by love' (Gal. 5:6), it is a faith which 'overcometh the world' (1 John 5:4), it is a faith which bringeth forth all manner of good works (Heb. 11). Let us now enter into detail, and show more specifically *wherein* lies the necessity for personal holiness.

1. *Our personal holiness is required by the very nature of God.* Holiness is the excellence and honour of the divine character. God is called 'rich in mercy' (Eph. 2:4), but 'glorious in holiness' (Exod. 15:11): his mercy is his treasure, but holiness is his glory. He swears by this perfection: 'Once have I sworn by my holiness' (Ps. 89:35). Over thirty times is he called 'The Holy One of Israel'. This is the superlative perfection for which the angels in heaven and the spirits of just men made perfect do so much admire God, crying 'Holy, holy, holy' (Isa. 6:3; Rev. 4:8). As gold, because it is the most excellent of the metals, is laid over inferior ones, so this divine excellency is laid upon all connected with him: his sabbath is 'holy' (Exod. 16:23), his sanctuary is 'holy'

(Exod. 15:13), his name is 'holy' (Ps. 99:3), all his works are 'holy' (Ps. 145:17). Holiness is the perfection of all his glorious attributes: his power is holy power, his mercy is holy mercy, his wisdom is holy wisdom.

Now the ineffable purity of the divine nature is everywhere in the Scriptures made the fundamental reason for the necessity of holiness in us. God makes the holiness of his own nature the ground of his demand for holiness in his people: 'For I am the LORD your God: ye shall therefore sanctify yourselves, and ye shall be holy, *for* I am holy' (Lev. 11:44). The same fundamental principle is transferred to the gospel, 'But as he which hath called you is holy, so be ye holy in all manner of conversation; because it is written, Be ye holy; for I am holy' (1 Pet. 1:15, 16). Thus God plainly lets us know that his nature is such as, unless we be sanctified, there can be no intercourse between him and us. 'For I am the Lord that bringeth you up out of the land of Egypt, *to be your God*: ye shall *therefore* be holy, for I am holy' (Lev. 11:45). Without personal holiness the relationship cannot be maintained that *he* should be our God and we should be *his* people.

God is 'of purer eyes than to behold evil, and canst not look on iniquity' (Hab. 1:13). Such is the infinite purity of his nature, that God cannot take any pleasure in lawless rebels, filthy sinners, the workers of iniquity. Joshua told the people plainly that if they continued in their sins, they could not serve the Lord, 'for he is an holy God' (Josh. 24:19). All the service of unholy people toward such a God is utterly lost and thrown away, because it is entirely inconsistent with his nature to accept of it. The apostle Paul reasons in the same manner when he says, 'Let us have grace, whereby we may serve God acceptably with reverence and godly fear: for our God is a consuming fire' (Heb. 12:28, 29). He lays his argument for the necessity of grace and holiness in the worship of God from the consideration of *the holiness of his nature* which, as a consuming fire, will devour that which is unsuited unto and inconsistent with it.

He who resolveth not to be holy must seek another god to worship and serve, for with the God of Scripture he will never find acceptance. The heathen of old realized this, and liking not to retain the knowledge of the true God in their hearts and minds (Rom. 1:28), and resolving to give up themselves unto all filthiness with greediness, they stifled their notions of the divine being and invented such 'gods' to themselves, as were unclean and wicked, that they might freely conform unto and serve *them* with satisfaction. God himself declares that men of corrupt lives have some secret hopes that he is not holy: 'Thou thoughtest that I was *altogether such an one as thyself*: but I will reprove thee' (Ps. 50:21). Others, today, while professing to believe in God's holiness, have such false ideas of his grace and mercy that they suppose he will accept them though they are unholy.

'Be ye holy, for I am holy.' Why? Because herein consists our conformity to God. We were originally created in the image and likeness of God, and that, for the substance of it, was *holiness* – therein consisted the privilege, blessedness, pre-eminence of man over all the lower creatures. Wherefore, without this conformity unto God, with the impress of his image and likeness upon the soul, we cannot stand in that relation unto God which was designed us in our creation. This we lost by the entrance of sin, and if there be not a way for us to acquire it again, we shall forever come short of the glory of God and the end of our creation. Now this is done by our becoming holy, for therein consists the renovation of God's image in us (Eph. 4:22-24 and cf. Col. 3:10). It is utterly vain for any man to expect an interest in God, while he does not earnestly endeavour after conformity to him.

To be sanctified is just as requisite as to be justified. He that thinks to come to enjoyment of God without holiness, makes him an unholy God, and puts the highest indignity imaginable upon him. There is no other alternative: we must either leave our sins, or our God. We may as easily reconcile heaven and hell, as easily take away all difference between light and darkness, good and evil, as procure acceptance for unholy persons with God. While it be true that our interest in God is not built upon our holiness, it is equally true that we have none without it. Many have greatly erred in concluding that, because piety and obedience are not meritorious, they can get to heaven without them. The free grace of God towards sinners by Jesus Christ by no means renders holiness needless and useless. Christ is not the minister of sin, but the maintainer of God's glory. He has not purchased for his people security *in* sin, but salvation *from* sin.

According to our growth in likeness unto God are our approaches unto glory. Each day both writer and reader is drawing nearer the end of his earthly course, and we do greatly deceive ourselves if we imagine that we are drawing nearer to heaven, while following those courses which lead only to hell. We are woefully deluded if we suppose that we are journeying towards glory, and yet are not growing in grace. The believer's glory, subjectively considered, will be his likeness to Christ (1 John 3:2), and it is the very height of folly for any to think that they shall love hereafter what now they hate. There is no other way of growing in the likeness of God *but in holiness*: thereby alone are we 'changed into the same image from glory to glory' (2 Cor. 3:18) – that is, from one degree of glorious grace to another, until by one last great change shall issue all grace and holiness in eternal glory.

But is not God ready to pardon and receive the greatest and vilest sinner who comes unto him by Christ? Is not his mercy so great and his grace so free that he will do so apart from *any consideration* of worth or righteousness of their own? If so, why insist so much on the indispensability

37

of holiness? This objection, though thousands of years old, is still made. If men must be holy, then carnal reasoners can see no need of grace: and they cannot see how God is gracious if men perish because they are unholy. Nothing seems more reasonable to carnal minds than that we may live in sin because grace has abounded. This is met by the apostle in Romans 6:1, where he subjoins the reasons why, notwithstanding the superaboundings of grace in Christ, there is an indispensable necessity why all believers should be holy. Without the necessity of holiness in us, grace would be disgraced. Note how when he proclaimed his name 'gracious and merciful', the Lord at once added, 'and will by no means clear the guilty' i.e. those who go on in their sins without regard unto obedience.

2. *Our personal holiness is required by the commands of God*. Not only is this so under the covenant of works, but the same is inseparably annexed under the covenant of grace. No relaxation unto the duty of holiness is granted by the gospel, nor any indulgence unto the least sin. The gospel is no less holy than the law, for both proceeded from the Holy One; and though provision be made for the pardon of a multitude of sins and for the acceptance of the Christian's imperfect obedience, yet the standard of righteousness is not lowered, for there is no abatement given by the gospel unto any duty of holiness nor any licence unto the least sin. The difference between those covenants is twofold: under that of works, all the duties of holiness were required as our righteousness before God, that we might be justified thereby (Rom. 10:5) – not so under grace; no allowance was made for the least degree of failure (James 2:10) – but, now, through the mediation of Christ, justice and mercy are joined together.

Under the gospel commands for universal holiness, respect is required unto three things. First, unto the *authority* of him who gives them. Authority is that which obligates unto obedience: see Malachi 1:6. Now he who commands us to be holy is our sovereign Lawgiver, with absolute right to prescribe that which he pleases, and therefore a non-compliance is a despising of the divine Legislator. To be under God's command to be holy, and then not to sincerely and earnestly endeavour always and in all things so to be, is to reject his sovereign authority over us, and to live in defiance of him. No better than *that* is the state of every one who does not make the pursuit of holiness his daily and chief concern. Forgetfulness of this, or failure to heed it as we ought, is the chief reason of our careless walking. *Our great safeguard is to keep our hearts and minds under a sense of the sovereign authority of God in his commands.*

Second, we must keep before our minds the *power* of him who commands us to be holy. 'There is one Lawgiver, who is able to save and to destroy' (James 4:12). God's commanding authority is accompanied with such power that he will eternally reward the obedient and eternally punish the disobedient. The commands of God are accompanied with promises of eternal bliss on the one hand, and of eternal misery on the other; and this will most certainly befall us according as we shall be found holy or unholy. Herein is to be seen a further reason for the indispensable necessity of our being holy: if we are not, then a holy and all-powerful God will damn us. A due respect unto God's promises and threatenings is a principal part of spiritual liberty: 'I am the Almighty God: walk before me, and be thou perfect' (Gen. 17:1): the way to walk uprightly is to ever bear in mind that he who requires it of us is Almighty God, under whose eyes we are continually. If, then, we value our souls, let us seek grace to act accordingly.

Third, respect is to be had unto the infinite *wisdom and goodness* of God. In his commands God not only maintains his sovereign authority over us, but also exhibits his righteousness and love. His commands are not the arbitrary edicts of a capricious despot, but the wise decrees of One who has our good at heart. His commands 'are not grievous' (1 John 5:3): they are not tyrannical restraints of our liberty, but are just, wholesome, and highly beneficial. It is to our great advantage to comply with them; it is for our happiness, both now and hereafter, that we obey them. They are a heavy burden only unto those who desire to be the slaves of sin and Satan: they are easy and pleasant unto all who walk with God. *Love for God carries with it a desire to please him,* and from Christ may be obtained that grace which will assist us thereto – but of this, more later.

3. *Our personal holiness is required by the Mediation of Christ.* One principal end of the design of God in sending his Son into the world was to recover us unto that state of holiness which we had lost: 'For this purpose the Son of God was manifested, that he might destroy the works of the devil' (1 John 3:8). Among the principal of the works of the devil was the infecting of our natures and persons with a principle of sin and enmity against God, and that evil work is not destroyed but by the introduction of a principle of holiness and obedience. The image of God in us was defaced by sin; the restoration of that image was one of the main purposes of Christ's mediation. Christ's great and ultimate design was to bring his people unto the enjoyment of God to his eternal glory, and this can only be by grace and holiness, by which we are made 'meet for the inheritance of the saints in light'.

Now the exercise of Christ's mediation is discharged under his threefold office. As to his priestly, the *immediate* effects were the making of satisfaction and reconciliation, but the *mediate* effects are our justification and sanctification: 'Who gave himself for us, that he might redeem us from all iniquity, and purify unto himself a peculiar people, zealous of good works' (Titus 2:14) – no *unholy* people, then, have any sure evidence of an interest in Christ's sacrifice. As to his prophetic office, this consists in his revelation to us of God's love and will: to make God known and to bring us into subjection unto him. At the very beginning of his prophetic ministry we find Christ restoring *the law* to its original purity – purging it from the corruptions of the Jews: Matthew 5. As to his kingly office, he subdues our lusts and supplies power for obedience. It is by these things we are to test ourselves. To live in known and allowed sin, and yet expect to be saved by Christ is the master deception of Satan.

From which of Christ's offices do I expect advantage? Is it from his *priestly*? Then has his blood cleansed me? Have I been made holy thereby? Have I been redeemed out of the world by it? Am I by it dedicated to God and his service? Is it from his *prophetic* office? Then have I effectually learned of him to 'deny ungodliness and worldly lusts, and to live soberly, righteously, and godly, in this present world?' (Titus 2:12). Has he instructed me unto *sincerity* in all my ways, in all my dealings with God and men? Is it from his *kingly* office? Then does he *actually* rule in me and over me? Has he delivered me from the power of Satan and caused me to take *his* yoke upon me? Has his sceptre broken the dominion of sin in me? Am I a loyal subject of his kingdom? If not, I have no rightful claim to a personal interest in his sacrifice. Christ died to procure holiness, not to secure an indulgence for unholiness.

4. *Our personal holiness is required in order to the glory of Christ.* If we are indeed his disciples, he has bought us with a price, and we are 'not our own', but his, and that to glorify him in soul and body because they are his: 1 Corinthians 6:19, 20. He died for us that we should not henceforth live unto ourselves, but unto him who redeemed us at such fearful

cost. How, then, are we to do this? *In our holiness* consists the principal part of that revenue of honour which the Lord Jesus requires and expects from his disciples in this world. Nothing glorifies him so much as our obedience; nothing is a greater grief and reproach to him than our disobedience. We are to witness before the world unto the holiness of his life, the heavenliness of his doctrine, the preciousness of his death, by a daily walk which 'shows forth HIS praises' (1 Peter 2:9). This is absolutely necessary if we are to glorify him in this scene of his rejection.

Nothing short of the *life* of Christ is our *example*: this is what the Christian is called to 'follow'. It is the life of Christ which it is his duty to express in his own, and he who takes up Christianity on any other terms woefully deceives his soul. No more effectual reproach can be cast upon the blessed name of the Lord Jesus than for his professing people to follow the lusts of the flesh, be conformed to this world, and heed the behests of Satan. We can only bear witness for the Saviour as we make his doctrine our rule, his glory our concern, his example our practice. Christ is honoured not by wordy expressions, but by a holy conversation. Nothing has done more to bring the gospel of Christ into reproach than the wicked lives of those who bear his name. If I am not living a holy and obedient life this shows that I am not 'for' Christ, but *against* him. (N.B. Much in this chapter is a condensation of John Owen on the same subject, Vol. 3, of his works.)

4

Its Problem

It should hardly be necessary for us to explain that when speaking of the *problem* of sanctification we refer not to such as unto God, but rather as it appears unto our feeble perceptions. But in these days it is not wise to take anything for granted, for not only are there some ready to make a man an offender for a word, if he fails to express himself to their satisfaction, but there are others who need to have the simplest terms defined unto them. No, it would be blasphemy to affirm that sanctification, or anything else, ever presented any problem to the great Jehovah: omniscience can never be confronted with any difficulty, still less an emergency. But to the Christian's finite understanding, deranged as it has been by sin, the problem of holiness is a very real and actual one; far more perplexing, we may add, than that presented by the subject of justification.

There are various subsidiary difficulties in sanctification, as we intimated in the fourth and fifth paragraphs of the introductory chapter, such as whether sanctification itself be a quality or a position, whether it be legal or experimental, whether it be absolute or progressive; all of which need to be cleared up in any satisfactory treatment of this theme. But far more intricate is the problem itself of how one who

43

is a moral leper can be fit to worship in the Sanctuary of God. Strange to say this problem is the acutest unto those who are the most spiritual. Self-righteous Pharisees and self-satisfied Laodiceans are in no wise troubled over the matter. Antinomians cut the knot (instead of untying it) and deny all difficulty, by asserting that the holiness of Christ is imputed to us. But those who realize God requires *personal* holiness, yet are conscious of their own filthiness, are deeply concerned thereupon.

Things are now, generally, at such a low ebb, that some of our readers may be surprised to find us making any reference at all to the *problem* of sanctification. In most places, today, either the doctrine taught is so inadequate and powerless, or the practice maintained is so defective, that few are likely to be exercised in conscience over the nature of that holiness without which none shall see the Lord. The claims of God are now so whittled down, the exalted standard which Scripture sets forth is so disregarded, *heart purity* (in which vital godliness so largely consists) is so little emphasized, that it is rare to find any concerned about their personal state. If there be some preachers zealously warning against the worthlessness of good works to save where there be no faith in Christ, there are far more who earnestly cry up an empty faith, which is unaccompanied by personal holiness and obedience.

Such a low standard of spiritual living now prevails, that comparatively few of the Lord's own people have any clear or disturbing conceptions of how far, far short they come of measuring up to the holy model which God has set before us in his Word. Such feeble and faulty ideals of Christian living now prevail that those who are preserved from the grosser evils which even the world condemns, are 'at ease in Zion'. So little is the fear of God upon souls, so faintly are the majority of professing Christians conscious of the plague of their own hearts, that in most quarters to speak about the *problem* of sanctification would be talking in an unknown tongue. A fearful miasma has settled down upon nine-tenths of Christendom, deadening the senses, blunting spiritual perceptions, paralysing endeavour after deeper personal piety, till almost anything is regarded as being acceptable unto God.

On the other hand, there is no doubt that some of us have intensified the problem, by creating for ourselves additional and needless difficulties, through erroneous ideas of what sanctification is or what it involves in this life. The writer has been personally acquainted with more than one who was in abject despair through failing – after the most earnest and resolute efforts – to attain unto a state which false teachers had told them was attainable in this life, and who terminated their mortal wretchedness by committing suicide; and it has long been a wonder to him that thousands more who heed such teachers do not act likewise. There is no need to multiply difficulties: scriptural sanctification is neither the eradication of sin, the purification of the carnal nature, nor even the partial putting to sleep of the 'flesh'; still less does it secure an exemption from the attacks and harassments of Satan.

Yet, on the other side, we must not minimize the problem, and reduce it to such simple proportions that we suppose a complete solution thereto is provided by merely affirming that Christ is our sanctification, and in himself the believing sinner remains unchanged to the end of his earthly course. If we die unholy in ourselves, then we are most assuredly lost for eternity, for only the 'pure in heart' shall ever see God (Matt. 5:8). What that purity of heart is, and how it is to be obtained, is the very real problem which sanctification raises. It is at the heart God looks (1 Sam. 16:7), and it is with the heart we need to be most concerned, for 'out of it are the issues of life' (Prov. 4:23). The severest woes were pronounced by Christ upon men not because their external

45

conduct was foul, but because *within* they were 'full of dead bones, and all uncleanness' (Matt. 23:27).

That personal holiness is absolutely essential for an entrance into heaven was shown at length in our last chapter, and that what men regard as the lesser pollutions of sin just as effectually exclude from the kingdom of God as do the most heinous crimes, is clear from 1 Corinthians 6:9-10. The question which forces itself upon us is, *How* shall men be sanctified so as to suit an infinitely pure God? That we must be justified before we can stand before a righteous God is no more obvious than that it is necessary that we must be sanctified so as to live in the presence of a holy God. But man is utterly without holiness; yea, he is impure, foul, filthy. The testimony of Scripture on this point is plain and full. 'They are *corrupt*, they have done abominable works, there is none that doeth good. The LORD looked down from heaven upon the children of men, to see if there were any that did understand, and seek God. They are all gone aside, they are all together become filthy' (Ps. 14:1-3).

The testimony of Scripture is that all men are vile and polluted; that they are, root and branch, source and stream, heart and life, not only disobedient, but *unholy*, and therefore *unfit* for God's purpose. The Lord Jesus who knew what was in man, makes this clear enough when, revealing with his own light that loathsome den, the human heart, he says, 'Out of the heart of men, proceed evil thoughts, adulteries, fornications, murders, thefts, covetousness, wickedness, deceit, lasciviousness, an evil eye, blasphemy, pride, foolishness: all these evil things come from within' (Mark 7:21-23). Nor must we forget that the confession of saints concerning themselves has always corresponded to God's testimony. David says, 'Behold, I was shapen in iniquity, and in sin did my mother conceive me' (Ps. 51). Job declared, 'Behold I am vile; I abhor myself.' Isaiah cried out, 'Woe is me, for I am undone; because I am a man of unclean lips ... for mine eyes have seen the King, the LORD of hosts.'

But the most remarkable confession of this absolute vileness is contained in an acknowledgement by the Old Testament church – a sentence which has been taken up by all believers as exactly expressing what they all have to say of their children by nature: 'But we are all as *an unclean thing*, and all our righteousnesses are as filthy rags' (Isa. 64:6). Strong language indeed is that, yet not one whit too strong to depict the mud and mire into which the Fall has brought us. If, then, when considering the doctrine of justification we found it appropriate – in view of man's self-will, lawlessness, and disobedience – to ask, 'How shall a man be just with God?' it is no less so now we are contemplating the doctrine of sanctification to inquire – in view of man's uncleanness and filthiness – *'Who* can bring a clean thing out of an unclean?' (Job 14:4).

We have no more power to make ourselves holy than we have to unmake or unbeing ourselves; we are no more able to cleanse our hearts, than we are to command or direct the winds. Sin in dominion is the 'plague' of the heart (1 Kings 8:38), and as no disease is so deadly as the plague, so there is no plague so deadly as *that of the heart.* 'Can the Ethiopian change his skin, or the leopard his spots? Then may ye also do good that are accustomed to do evil' (Jer. 13:23). The proud cannot make himself humble; the carnal cannot force himself to become spiritual; the earthly man can no more transform himself into a heavenly man than he can make the sun go backward or the earth fly upward. Sanctification is a work altogether above the powers of human nature: alas that this is so little realized today.

Even among those preachers who desire to be regarded as orthodox, who do not deny the Fall as a historical fact, few among them perceive the dire effects and extent thereof. *'Bruised* by the Fall,' as one popular hymn puts it, states the

47

truth far too mildly; yea, entirely misstates it. Through the breach of the first covenant all men have lost the image of God, and now bear the image of the devil (John 8:44). The whole of their faculties are so depraved that they can neither think (2 Cor. 3:5), speak, nor do anything truly good and acceptable unto God. They are by birth, altogether unholy, unclean, loathsome and abominable in nature, heart, and life; and it is altogether beyond their power to change themselves.

Not only so, but the curse of the law lying upon them has severed all spiritual relation between God and them, cutting off all communion and communication with heaven. The driving from the Garden of Eden of our first parents and the establishment of the cherubim with the flaming sword at its entrance, denoted that in point of justice they were barred from all sanctifying influences reaching them – that being the greatest benefit man is capable of, as assimilating him to God himself or rendering him like him. The *curse* has fixed a gulf between God and fallen creatures, so that sanctifying influences cannot pass from him unto them, any more than their unholy desires and prayers can pass unto him. It is written, 'The sacrifice of the wicked is an abomination to the LORD' (Prov. 15:8). And again, 'The thoughts of the wicked are an abomination to the LORD' (v. 26).

It has, then, been rightly said that our sanctification 'is no less a mystery than our justification' (Thomas Boston). As the depravity of human nature has always been so manifest that it could not escape notice even in the world, so in all ages men have been seeking to discover a remedy for the same, and have supposed a cure could be achieved by a right use of their rational faculties. But the outcome has always been, at best, but an outward show and semblance of sanctification, going under the name of 'mortal virtue'. But so far is that from meeting the requirements of him who is Light, that men themselves, once their eyes are (in any measure) anointed with heavenly eyesalve, perceive their mortal virtue to be as 'filthy rags'. Until men are regenerate and act from a principle of grace in the heart, all their actions are but imitations of real obedience and piety, as an ape would mimic a man.

It is a common error of those that are unregenerate to seek to reform their conduct without any realization that their *state* must be changed before their lives can possibly be changed from sin to righteousness. The tree itself must be made good, before its fruit can possibly be good. As well attempt to make a watch go, whose mainspring is broken, by washing its face and polishing its back, as for one under the curse of God to produce any works acceptable to him. That was the great mistake Nicodemus laboured under: he supposed that *teaching* was all he needed, so that he might adjust his walk to the acceptance of heaven. But to him the Lord Jesus declared, 'Marvel not that I said unto thee, Ye must be born again' (John 3:7): that was only another way of saying, Nicodemus, you cannot perform spiritual works before you possess a spiritual nature and a spiritual nature cannot be had until you are born again.

Multitudes have laboured with great earnestness to subdue their evil propensities, and have struggled long and hard to bring their inward thoughts and affections into conformity with the law of God. They have sought to abstain from all sins, and to perform every known duty. They have been so devout and intent that they have undermined their health, and were so fervent in their zeal that they were ready to kill their bodies with fastings and mascerations, if only they might kill their sinful lusts. They were strongly convinced that holiness was absolutely necessary unto salvation, and were so deeply affected with the terrors of damnation, as to forsake the world and shut themselves up in convents and monasteries; yet all the while ignorant of the *mystery* of sanctification – that *a new state* MUST precede *a new life*.

It is positively asserted by divine inspiration that, 'They that are in the flesh cannot please God' (Rom. 8:8). Alas, how few understand the meaning of those words 'in the flesh'; how many suppose they only signify, to be inordinately addicted to the baser passions. Whereas, to be 'in the flesh' is to be in a state of nature – fallen, depraved, alienated from the life of God. To be 'in the flesh' is not simply being a personal transgressor of God's holy law, but is *the cause* of all sinfulness and sinning. The 'flesh' is the very *nature* of man as corrupted by the fall of Adam, and propagated from him to us in that corrupt state by natural generation. To be 'in the flesh' is also being in complete subjection to the power of the devil, who is the certain conqueror of all who attempt to fight him in their own strength or with his own weapons. The flesh can no more be brought to holiness by man's most vehement endeavours, than he can bring a dead carcass to life by chafing and rubbing it.

The varied elements which entered into the problem of justification were: God's law requires from us perfect obedience to its statutes; this we have utterly failed to render; we are therefore under the condemnation and curse of the law; the Judge himself is inflexibly just, and will by no means clear the guilty: how, then, can men be shown mercy without justice being flouted? The elements which enter into the problem of sanctification are: the law requires inward as well as outward conformity to it: but we are born into this world with a nature that is totally depraved, and can by no means be brought into subjection to the law (Rom. 8:7). God himself is ineffably pure, how then can a moral leper be admitted into his presence? We are utterly without holiness, and can no more make ourselves holy than the Ethiopian can change his skin. Even though a holy nature be imparted by regeneration, how can one with the flesh, unchanged, within him, draw near as a worshipper unto the heavenly sanctuary? How can I as a person possibly regard myself as holy, while conscious that I am full of sin? How can I honestly profess to have a 'pure heart', while realizing that a sea of corruption still rages within me? If my *state* must be changed before anything in my *life* is acceptable to God, what can I possibly do? – I cannot unmake myself. If *I* know that I am polluted and vile, and utterly unsuited unto the thrice holy God, how much less can *he* regard me as fit for his presence?

5

Its Solution

In connection with the grand truth of sanctification there is both a mystery and a problem: the former relates to the unregenerate; the latter is what exercises so deeply the regenerate. That which is hidden from the understanding of the natural man is, why his best performances are unacceptable unto God, no matter how earnestly and devoutly they be done. Even though he be informed that the tree must be made good if its fruit is to be wholesome, in other words, that his very *state* and *nature* must first be made acceptable unto God before any of his *works* can be so, he has not the remotest idea of how this is to be accomplished. But that which perplexes the spiritual man is, how one who is still full of sin may justly regard his state and nature as being acceptable unto God, and how one who is a mass of corruption within can honestly claim to be holy. As the Lord is pleased to enable we will consider each in turn.

The natural man is quite ignorant of the mystery of sanctification. Though he may – under the spur of conscience, the fear of hell, or from desire to go to heaven – be very diligent in seeking to conquer the activities of indwelling sin and exceedingly zealous in performing every known duty, yet he is quite in the dark as to why his *state* must be changed before his *actions* can be acceptable unto God.

That upon which he is unenlightened is, that it is not *the matter* which makes a work good and pleasing to God, but *the principles* from which that work proceeds. It is true that the conscience of the natural man distinguishes between good and evil, and religious instruction may educate him to do much which is right and avoid much that is wrong; nevertheless, his actions are not done out of gratitude and in a spirit of loving obedience, but out of fear and from a servile spirit; and therefore are they like fruit ripened by art and forced in the hothouse, rather than normally by the genial rays of the sun.

'Now the end (design) of the commandment (or law) is charity out of a pure heart, and a good conscience, and faith unfeigned' (1 Tim. 1:5). Nothing less than this will meet the divine requirements. Only those actions are pleasing to God which have respect unto his commandment, which proceed from gratitude unto him for his goodness, and where faith has respect unto his promised acceptance and blessing. No works are approved of heaven except they possess these qualities. A sense of duty must sway the conscience, disinterested affection must move the heart, and faith in exercise must direct the actions. Hence, should I be asked why I do thus and so? the answer should be, Because God has commanded it. And if it be further enquired, And why such earnestness and affection? the answer ought to be, Because God requires my best, and I desire to honour him with the same. Obedience respects God's authority; love, his kindness; faith, his bounty or reward.

'Whether therefore ye eat, or drink, or whatsoever ye do, do all to the glory of God' (1 Cor. 10:31). This must be our design – the glory of God – if our actions are to meet with his approval. Whether it be the discharge of our temporal duties, the performing of deeds of charity and kindness, or acts of piety and devotion, they must be executed with this aim: that *God* may be honoured by our conformity to his revealed will. The natural man, when in sore straits, will cry fervently unto God, but it is only that *his* wants be supplied. Many will contribute liberally of their means to the relief of sufferers, but it is to be 'seen of men' (Matt. 6:1). People are religious on the Sabbath and attend public worship, but it is either to satisfy an uneasy conscience or in the hope of earning heaven thereby.

From what has been said above it should be clear that the best deeds of the unregenerate fall far short of the divine requirements. The actions of the natural man cannot receive the approbation of heaven, because *God* is neither the beginning nor the end of them: love for him is not their spring, glorifying him is not their aim. Instead, they issue from the workings of corrupt self, and they have in view only the advancement of self. Nor can it be otherwise. Water will not rise above its own level, or flow uphill. A pure stream cannot issue from an impure fountain. 'That which is born of the flesh is flesh' (John 3:6), and will never be anything but flesh: educate, refine, religionize the flesh all we may, it can never become spirit. The man himself must be sanctified before his actions are purified.

But how shall men be sanctified so as to be suited unto the presence of an infinitely pure God? By nature they are utterly without holiness: they are 'corrupt, filthy, an unclean thing'. They have no more power to make themselves holy than they have to create a world. We could tame a tiger from the jungle far more easily than we could our lusts. We might empty the ocean more quickly than we could banish pride from our souls. We might melt marble more readily than our hard hearts. We might purge the sea of salt more easily than we could our beings of sin. 'For though thou wash thee with nitre, and take thee much soap, yet thine iniquity is marked before me, saith the Lord God' (Jer. 2:22).

Why 'when we were in our best condition by nature, when we were in the state of original holiness, when we were in Adam vested with the image of God, we preserved it not. How much less likely then is it, that now, in the state of lapsed and depraved nature, it is in our power to restore ourselves, to reintroduce the image of God into our souls, and that in a far more eminent manner than it was at first created by God? What needed all that contrivance of infinite wisdom and grace for the reparation of our nature by Jesus Christ, if holiness, wherein it doth consist, be in our power, and educed out of the natural faculties of our souls? There can be no more fond imagination befall the minds of men, than that defiled nature is able to cleanse itself, or depraved nature to rectify itself, or we, who have lost that image of God which he created in us, and with us, should create it again in ourselves by our own endeavours' (John Owen).

Yet, let it be pointed out that this impotency to measure up to the requirements of God is no mere innocent infirmity, but a highly culpable thing, which greatly aggravates our vileness and adds to our guilt. Our inability to measure up to the standard of personal piety which God has appointed, lies not in a lack of executive power or the needful faculties, but in the want of a willing mind and a ready heart to practise true holiness. If men in a natural state had a hearty love and liking to true holiness, and a fervent and sincere endeavour to practise it, and yet failed in the event, then they might under some pretence plead for this excuse (as many do), that they are compelled to sin by an inevitable necessity. But the fact is that man's impotency lies in his own *obstinancy* – 'Ye will not come to me' (John 5:40) said the Lord Jesus.

Inability to pay a debt does not excuse a debtor who has recklessly squandered his estate; nor does drunkenness excuse the mad or violent actions of a drunkard, but rather aggravates his crime. God has not lost his right to command, even though man through his wickedness has lost his power to obey. Because the flesh 'lusteth against the Spirit'

(Gal. 5:17), that is far from an extenuation for not being in subjection to him. Because 'every one that doeth evil *hateth* the light', that is far from justifying them because they 'loved darkness' (John 3:19, 20); yea, as the Saviour there so plainly and solemnly states, it only serves to heighten their criminality – 'This is *the* condemnation'. Then 'How much more abominable and filthy is man, which drinketh iniquity like water?' (Job 15:16), that cannot practise holiness because he will not.

It is because men do not *make a right use* of their faculties that they are justly condemned. The soul in an unsanctified person is not dead, but is a living and acting principle; and therefore it is able to understand, desire, will, reason, and improve its opportunities, or redeem the time. Though the natural man is unable to work grace in his own heart, yet he is able to attend and wait upon the means of grace. An unsanctified person may as well go to hear a sermon as attend a theatre: he has the same eyes for reading the Scriptures as the newspaper or a novel: he may as well associate himself with those who fear an oath, as with those who delight to blaspheme that Name at which all should tremble. In the day of judgment unsanctified persons will be damned not for *cannots*, but for *will nots*.

Men complain that they cannot purify themselves, that they cannot cease from sin, that they cannot repent, that they cannot believe in Christ, that they cannot live a holy life. But if only they were honest, if they were duly humbled, if they sincerely grieved over the awful hold which sin has obtained upon them, they would fly to the throne of grace, they would cry unto God day and night for him to break the chains which bind them, deliver them from the power of Satan and translate them into the kingdom of his dear Son. If they were but sincere in their complaint of inability, they would go to God and beg him to sprinkle clean water upon them, put his Spirit within them, and give them a new heart, so that they might walk in his statutes and keep his judgements (Ezek. 36:25-28). And it is just because they will not, that their blood justly lies upon their own heads.

'Cleanse your hands, ye sinners; and purify your hearts, ye double-minded' (James 4:8). Outward separation from that which is evil and polluting is not sufficient: purity of heart is also indispensable. 'Behold, thou desirest truth in the *inward* parts' (Ps. 51:6). The divine law not only prohibits stealing, but also insists 'thou shall not covet', which is a lusting of our souls rather than an external act. Holiness *of nature* is required by the law, for how else shall a man love the Lord his God with all his heart, soul, mind, and strength, and his neighbour as himself? God is essentially holy by nature, and nothing can be so contrary to him as an unholy nature. Nothing can be so contrary as opposite natures. How can a wolf and a lamb, or a vulture and a dove, dwell together? 'What fellowship hath righteousness with unrighteousness? and what communion hath light with darkness? and what concord hath Christ with Belial?' (2 Cor. 6:14, 15).

How, then, is this mystery cleared up? By what method, or in what way, have the sanctified become blest with a nature which makes them meet for the ineffable presence of God? By what process does the evil tree become good, so that its fruit is wholesome and acceptable? Obviously, we cannot here supply the full answer to these questions, or we should be anticipating too much that we desire to bring out in later chapters. But we will endeavour to now indicate, at least, the direction in which and the lines along which this great mystery is cleared – lines which most assuredly would never have entered our hearts and minds to so much as conceive; but which once they are viewed by anointed eyes, are seen to be divine and satisfying. The Lord graciously assist us to steer clear of the rocks of error and guide us into the clear and refreshing waters of the truth.

As we have shown, it was quite impossible – though it was their bounden duty – for those whom God sanctifies to personally answer the requirements of his holy law: 'Who can say, I have made my heart clean, I am pure from my sin?' (Prov. 20:9). Wherefore, for the satisfaction of the law, which requires absolute purity of nature, it was settled as one of the articles in the Everlasting Covenant, that Christ, the Representative of all who would be sanctified, should be a Man of an untainted and perfectly pure nature, which fully met the requirements of the law: 'For such an High Priest became us – holy, harmless, undefiled, separate from sinners' (Heb. 7:26). The meeting of that requirement necessitated two things: first, that the Head of his people should be born with a holy human nature; second, that he should retain that holiness of nature inviolate unto the end. Let us consider, briefly, each of these separately.

There was a holy nature given to Adam as the Root of mankind, to be kept by him and transmitted to his posterity by natural generation. Upon that ground the law requires all men to be born holy, and pronounces them unclean and 'children of wrath' (Eph. 2:3) in the contrary. But how can this demand be met by those who are born in sin? They cannot enter again into their mother's womb, and be born a second time without sin. Even so, the law will not abate its demand. Wherefore it was provided that Christ, the last Adam, should, as the Representative and Root of his spiritual seed, be born perfectly holy; that whereas they brought a sinful nature into the world with them, he should be born 'that *holy* thing' (Luke 1:35). Consequently, in the reckoning of the law all believers are born holy in the last Adam. They are said to be 'circumcised' by the circumcision of Christ (Col. 2:11), and circumcision necessarily presupposes *birth*!

But more was required. It was necessary that the Second Man should preserve his holy nature free from all spot or defilement, as he passed through this world of sin. The law not only demands holiness of nature, but also that the purity and integrity of that nature be preserved. Wherefore to satisfy this demand, it was provided that the believers' federal Head should preserve his ineffable purity unstained. 'He shall not fail' (Isa. 42:4). The first man did fail: the fine gold soon became dim: the holiness of his nature was quickly extinguished by sin. But the Second Man failed not: neither man nor devil could corrupt him. He preserved the holiness of his nature unstained, even to the end of his life. And so of his sanctified, viewing them in himself, he declares, 'Thou art all fair, my love; there is no spot in thee' (Song of Songs 4:7).

But while that completely meets the judicial side, satisfying the demands of the law, something more was yet required to satisfy the heart of God and meet the experimental needs of his people. In view of their being actually defiled in Adam when he sinned, they are defiled in their own persons so that not only is his guilt imputed to them, but his corruption is imparted to them in the nature they have received from him by generation. Therefore, not only were the elect legally born holy in Christ their Head, but from him they also receive a holy nature: it is written, 'The first man Adam was made a living soul; the last Adam was made a quickening Spirit' (1 Cor. 15:45). This is accomplished by that gracious and supernatural working of the third person in the Godhead, whereby the elect are vitally united to their head so that 'he that is joined unto the Lord is *one spirit*' (1 Cor. 6:17).

'Therefore if any man be in Christ, he is a new creature: old things are passed away; behold, all things are become new' (2 Cor. 5:17). Our being united to Christ, through the Spirit, by faith, makes us partakers of the same spiritual and holy nature with him, as really and as actually as Eve (type of the Church) was made of one nature with Adam, being bone of his bone and flesh of his flesh. Because believers are united to Christ the Holy One, they are 'sanctified in Christ Jesus' (1 Cor. 1:2). The believer being one with Christ is made 'a new creature', because he is such a Stock as changes the graft into its own nature: 'If the Root be holy, so are the branches' (Rom. 11:16). The same Spirit which Christ received 'without measure' (John 3:34) is communicated to the members of his body, so that it can be said, 'Of his fullness have all we received, and grace for grace (John 1:16). Being united to Christ by faith, and through the communication of the quickening Spirit from Christ unto him, the believer is thereupon not only justified and reconciled to God, but sanctified, made meet for the inheritance of the saints in light, and made an heir of God.

Its Solution (Completed)

At the beginning of this chapter it was pointed out that in connection with the grand truth of sanctification there is both a mystery and a problem: the former relating to the unregenerate, the latter causing concern to the regenerate. That which is hidden from the knowledge of the natural man is, why his best works are unacceptable to God. Tell him that *all* his actions – no matter how carefully and conscientiously, diligently and devoutly, executed – are rejected by God, and that is something entirely above the reach of his understanding. He knows not that his breaking of the law in Adam has brought in a breach between himself and God, so that while that breach remains, the favour of God cannot flow out of him, nor his prayers or offerings pass in to God. The Lord will no more receive anything at the hands of the natural man than he would have respect unto the offering of Cain (Gen. 4). And had he left all men in their natural estate, this would have held true of the whole race until the end of time.

Inasmuch as all men were given a holy nature – created in the image and likeness of God – in their representative and root, to be transmitted to them by him, *before* the law was given to Adam, it follows that the law requires a holy nature from each of us, and pronounces a curse wherever it finds the opposite. Though we are actually born into this world in a state of corruption and filth (Ezek. 16:3-6, etc.), yet the law will not abate its just demands upon us. In consequence of the sin which indwells us – which is so much a part and parcel of ourselves that everything we do is defiled thereby – we are thoroughly unable to render unto the law that obedience which it requires; for while we are alienated from the life of God, it is impossible that any outward acts of compliance with the law's statutes can proceed from those principles which it alone can approve of, namely, disinterested love and faith unfeigned. Consequently, the state of the natural man, considered in himself, is entirely beyond hope.

The provision made by the manifold wisdom and sovereign grace of God to meet the desperate needs of his people was stipulated for in terms of the Everlasting Covenant. There it was agreed upon by the Eternal Three that the Mediator should be the Son of man, yet, that his humanity should be not only entirely free from every taint of original sin, but should be purer than that of Adam's even when his Creator pronounced him 'very good'. This was accomplished by the supernatural operation of the Holy Spirit in the virgin birth, and by the Son of God taking into personal union with himself 'that holy thing' which was to be born of Mary. Inasmuch as Christ, the God-man Mediator, entered this world not as a private Person, but as a public, as the Representative and Head of God's elect, in the reckoning of the law they were born holy in their Surety and Sponsor, and so fully measure up to its requirements. Christ and his mystical body have never been viewed apart by the law.

But this, unspeakably blessed though it be, was not all. A perfect legal standing only met half of the need of God's elect: in addition, their *state* must be made to accord with their standing. This also has been provided for by the measureless love of the God of all grace. He so ordered that, just as the guilt of Adam was imputed to all for whom he acted, so the righteousness of Christ should be imputed to all for whom he transacted: and, that just as spiritual death – with all its corrupting effects – should be transmitted by Adam to all his posterity, so the spiritual life of Christ – with all its gracious influences – should be communicated to all his seed. As they received a sinful and impure nature from their natural head, so the sanctified receive a sinless and pure nature from their spiritual Head. Consequently, as they have borne the image of the earthy, so they shall bear the image of the heavenly.

Some of our readers may, perhaps, conclude that all difficulty in connection with this aspect of our subject has now been disposed of, but a little reflection on the part of the believer should soon remind him that the most perplexing point of all has yet to be cleared up. Though it be true that every essential requirement of the law has been met for the sanctified by their glorious Head, so that the law righteously views them as holy in him; and though it be true that at regeneration they receive from Christ, by the Spirit, a new and holy nature, like unto his; yet the old nature remains, and remains unchanged, unimproved. Yea, to them it seems that the carnal nature in them is steadily growing worse and worse, and more active and defiling every day they live. They are painfully conscious of the fact that sin not only remains in them, but that it pollutes their desires, thoughts, imaginations, and acts; and to prevent its uprisings they are quite powerless.

This presents to an honest heart and a sensitive conscience a problem which is most acute, for how can those who abhor themselves be pleasing unto the thrice holy One? How can those conscious of their filthiness and vileness possibly be fit to draw nigh unto him who is ineffably and infinitely pure? The answer which some have returned to this agonized enquiry – based upon an erroneous deduction from the words of Paul 'it is no more I that do it, but sin that dwelleth in me' (Rom. 7:20) – will by no means satisfy them. To say it is not the regenerate person, but only the flesh in him, which sins, is to invent a distinction which repudiates the Christian's responsibility, and which affords no relief to a quickened conscience. Scripture is far too plain on this point to justify a mistake: Old and New Testament alike insist it is *the person* who sins – 'against thee ... have I sinned' (Ps. 51). Paul himself concludes Romans 7 by saying, 'O wretched man that *I* am!'

Where other matters are concerned, men have more sense than to fall back upon such a distinction as some modern theologians are so fond of insisting upon: it never occurs to them to argue thus in connection with temporal things. Imagine one before a judge, who was charged with theft, acknowledging his offence, but disowning all responsibility and culpability on the ground that it was his 'evil nature' and *not himself* which did the stealing! Surely the judge would be in a quandary to decide whether prison or the madhouse was the right place to send him. This reminds us of an incident wherein a 'Bishop' was guilty of blasphemy in the House of Lords (where all 'Bishops' have seats). Being rebuked by his manservant, he replied, 'It was the "lord" and not the "bishop" who cursed.' His servant responded, 'When the devil gets the "lord" where will the "bishop" be!' Beware, my reader, of seeking to clear yourself by throwing the blame upon your 'nature'.

Somewhere else, then, than in any supposed distinction between the sanctified person and his old nature, must the solution to our problem be sought. When one who has been walking with God is tripped up by some temptation and falls into sin, or when indwelling corruption surges up and (for the time being) obtains the mastery over him, he is painfully aware of the fact; and that which exercises him the most is not only that he has sinned against the One who is nearer and dearer to him than all else, but that his communion with him is broken, and that he is no longer morally fit to come into his sacred presence. Whilst his knowledge of the gospel may be sufficient to allay any haunting fears of the penal consequences of his sins, yet this does not remove the defilement from his conscience. This is one important respect in which the unregenerate and regenerate differ radically: when the former sins it is the *guilt* (and punishment) which most occupies his thoughts; but when the latter, it is the *defiling* effects which most exercise his heart.

There are two things in sin, inseparably connected and yet clearly distinguishable, namely, its criminality and its pollution. The pollution of sin is that property of it whereby it is directly opposed unto the holiness of God, and which God expresseth his holiness to be contrary unto. Therefore it is said, he is 'of purer eyes than to behold evil, and canst not look on iniquity' (Hab. 1:13) – it is a vile and loathsome sight to him who is the Light. Hence doth he use that pathetic entreaty, 'Oh, do not this abominable thing that I hate' (Jer. 44:4). It is with respect unto his own holiness that God sets forth sin by the names of everything which is offensive, objectionable, repulsive, abominable. Consequently, when the Holy Spirit convicts of sin, he imparts such a sight and sense of the filth of sin, that sinners blush, are ashamed, are filled with confusion of face, are abased in their own esteem, and abashed before God.

As we are taught the guilt by our own *fear*, which is the inseparable adjunct of it, so we are taught the filth of sin by our own *shame*, which unavoidably attends it. Under the typical economy God not only appointed sacrifices to make atonement for the guilt of sin, but also gave various ordinances for purification or ceremonial cleansing from the pollution thereof. In various ways, during Old Testament times, God instructed his people concerning the spiritual defilement of sin: the distinction between clean and unclean animals, the different natural distempers which befoul the body, the isolating of the leper, the accidental touching of the dead which rendered people religiously unclean by the law, are cases in point. All of them pre-figured internal and spiritual pollution, and hence the whole work of sanctification is expressed by 'a fountain opened ... for sin and for uncleanness' (Zech. 13:1) – that is, for the purging away of them.

So inseparable is moral pollution from sin, and a sense of shame from a consciousness of the pollution, that whenever a soul is truly convicted of sin, there is always a painful sense of this filthiness, accompanied by personal shame. Only as this is clearly apprehended, are we able to understand the true nature of sanctification. The spiritual comeliness of the soul consists in its conformity to God. Grace gives beauty: hence it is said of Christ that he is 'Fairer (or 'more beautiful') than the children of men', and that beauty consisted in his being made in the image of God, which constituted the whole harmony and symmetry of his nature, all his faculties and actions having respect unto God. Therefore, that which is contrary to the image of God – depravity, and contrary to grace – sin, hath in it a deformity which mars the soul, destroys its comeliness, disrupts its order, and brings deformity, ugliness, vileness.

Whatever is contrary to holiness or the image of God on the soul is base, unworthy, filthy. Sin dishonours and degrades the soul, filling it with shame. The closer we are permitted to walk with God and the more we see ourselves in his light, the more conscious are we of the deformity of sin and of our baseness. When our eyes were first opened to see our spiritual nakedness, how hideous did we appear unto ourselves, and what a sense of our pollution we had! That was but the reflex of God's view, for he abhors, loathes, and esteems as an abominable thing whatever is contrary to his holiness. Those who are made 'partakers of the divine nature' (2 Pet. 1:4), do, according to their measure, but see themselves with *God's* eyes, as wretched, naked, shameful, loathsome, hideous and abominable creatures; and therefore do they, with Job, 'abhor' themselves.

The last four paragraphs are, in part, a condensation from John Owen; and from them we may clearly perceive that it is they who are truly sanctified and holy, who are the most deeply sensible of the root of corruption which still remains within them, and which is ever springing up and producing that which defiles them; and therefore do they greatly bewail their pollutions, as that which is most dishonouring to God and most disturbing to their own peace; and earnestly do they endeavour after the mortification of it. A remarkable corroboration is found in the fact that the most godly and holy have been the very ones who most strongly affirmed their sinfulness and most loudly bewailed the same. It was one whom God himself declared to be a 'perfect (sincere) and an upright man, one that feareth God, and escheweth evil' (Job 1:8) who declared 'Behold, I am vile' (40:4). It was one 'greatly beloved' of God (Dan. 10:19), who acknowledged 'my comeliness was turned in me into corruption' (10:8). It was he who was caught up to the third heaven and then returned again to earth who moaned, 'O wretched man that I am! who shall deliver me from the body of this death?' (Rom. 7:24).

From the quotations just made from the personal confessions of some of the most eminent of God's saints, it is perfectly plain to any simple soul that a 'pure heart' cannot signify one from which all sin has been removed, nor can their language possibly be made to square with the utopian theory that the carnal nature is eradicated from any believer in this life. Indeed it cannot; and none but they who are completely blinded by Satan would ever affirm such a gross absurdity and palpable lie. But this requires us now to define and describe *what* a 'pure heart' consists of, according to the scriptural meaning. And in our efforts to supply this, we shall have to try and guard against two evils: providing a pillow for empty professors to comfortably rest upon; and stating things in such a way that hope would be killed in the regenerate.

First, a 'pure heart' is one which has experienced 'the washing of regeneration, and renewing of the Holy Ghost' (Titus 3:5). That takes place at the new birth, and is maintained by the Spirit throughout the Christian's life. All that this involves we cannot now state at any length. But, negatively, it includes the purifying of the believer's understanding, so that it is no longer fatally blinded by Satan, but is supernaturally illumined by the Spirit: in consequence, the vanity of worldly things is now perceived. The mind is, in great measure, freed from the pollution of error, and this by the shining in of the light of God's truth. It includes, negatively, the cleansing of the affections, so that sin is no longer loved but loathed, and God is no longer shrunk from and avoided, but sought after and desired.

From the positive side, there is communicated to the soul at regeneration a nature or principle which contains within itself pure desires, pure intentions, and pure roots of actions. The fear of God is implanted, and the love of God is shed abroad in the heart. In consequence, the soul is made to pant after God, yearn for conformity to his will, and seeks to please him in all things. And hence it is that the greatest grief of the Christian arises from the hindering of his spiritual longings and the thwarting of his spiritual aspirations. A pure heart is one that loathes impurity, and whose heaviest burden is the realization that such an ocean of foul waters still indwells him, constantly casting up their mire and dirt, polluting all he does. A 'pure heart' therefore, is one which *makes conscience* of foolish, vile imaginations, and evil desires. It is one which grieves over pride and discontent, mourns over unbelief, and enmity, weeps in secret over unholiness.

Second, a 'pure heart' is one which has been 'sprinkled from an evil conscience' (Heb. 10:22). An 'evil conscience' is one which accuses of guilt and oppresses because of unpardoned sin. Its possessor dreads the prospect of the day of judgment, and seeks to banish all thoughts of it from his mind. But a conscience to which the Spirit has graciously applied the atoning blood of Christ obtains peace of mind, and has confidence to draw nigh unto God: in consequence, superstition, terror and torment is removed, and an aversion to God is displaced by a joy in God. Hence, also, third, we read 'purifying their hearts by faith' (Acts 15:9). As unbelief is a principle which defiles, so faith is a principle which purges, and that, because of *the object which it lay holds of*. Faith looks away from self to Christ, and is enabled to realize that his blood 'cleanseth us from all sin' (1 John 1:7).

Every Christian, then, has a 'pure' heart in the particulars given above. But every Christian does not have a 'clean' heart (Ps. 51:10). That which pollutes the heart of a Christian is *unjudged sin*. Whenever sin is *allowed* by us, communion with God is broken, and pollution can only be removed, and communion restored, by genuine repentance – a condemning of ourselves, a mourning over the sin, and unsparing confession of the same, accompanied by a fervent desire and sincere resolution not to be overtaken by it again. The willing allowance and indulgence of any known sin cannot exist with a clean heart. Rightly, then, did John Owen say *of repentance*: 'It is as necessary unto the continuance of spiritual life as faith itself.' After the repentance and confession, there must be a fresh (and constant) recourse unto that Fountain which has been 'opened for sin and for uncleanness', a fresh application by faith of the cleansing blood of Christ: pleading its merits and efficacy before God.

In chapters six and seven we have sought to answer the questions at the close of the fifth chapter. We have met every demand of the law in the person of our Surety. We are made meet for the inheritance of the saints in light, because all the value of Christ's cleansing blood is reckoned to our account. We are capacitated to draw nigh unto God now, because the Holy Spirit has communicated to us the very nature of Christ himself. By faith we may regard ourselves as holy in Christ. By regeneration we have received a 'pure heart': proof of which is, we hate all impurity, although there is still that in us which delights in nothing else. We are to maintain communion with God by cleansing our own hearts (Ps. 73:13), and that, through constant mortification, and the daily and unsparing judgment of all known sin in and from us.

6
Its Nature

We have now reached what is, in several respects, the most important aspect of our theme. It is very necessary that we should seek after a clear and comprehensive view of the character of sanctification itself, what it really consists of; or, at best, our thoughts concerning it will be confused. Since holiness is, by general consent, the sum of all moral excellence, and the highest and most necessary attainment, it is of the utmost moment that we should well understand its real nature and be able to distinguish it from all counterfeits. How can it be discovered whether or not *we* have been sanctified, unless we really know what sanctification actually is? How can we truly cultivate holiness, until we have ascertained the real substance or essence of holiness? A right apprehension of the nature of sanctification or holiness is a great aid to the understanding of much in the Scriptures, to the forming of right conceptions of the divine perfections, and to the distinguishing of true religion from all that is false.

We have also now reached what is the most difficult and intricate aspect of our many-sided subject. The task of defining and describing the nature of sanctification is by no means a simple one. This is due, partly, to the many different aspects and angles which have to be borne in mind, if anything like a comprehensive conception is to be obtained. Scripture speaks of the believer being sanctified by God the Father; other passages speak of being sanctified by Christ and by his sacrifice; still others of being sanctified by the Spirit, by the Word, by faith, by chastisements. Of course these do not refer to so many different sanctifications, but to the various branches of one complete sanctification; which, nevertheless, need to be kept distinctly in our minds. Some Scriptures present sanctification as an objective thing, others as subjective. Sometimes sanctification is viewed as complete, at others as incomplete and progressive. These varied phases of our subject will pass under review in later chapters.

As we have consulted the works of others on this subject, we have been struck by the paucity of their remarks on *the nature* of sanctification. While many writers have treated at length on the meaning of the term itself, the manner in which this gift has been provided for the believer, the work of the Spirit in imparting the same, the varying degrees in which it is manifested in this life, yet few indeed have entered into a clear description of what holiness actually *is*. Where false conceptions have been mercifully avoided, yet, in most cases, only partial and very inadequate views of the truth thereon have been presented. It is our conviction that failure at *this* point, inattention to this most vital consideration, has been responsible, more than anything else, for the conflicting opinions which prevail so widely among professing Christians. A mistake at this point opens the door for the entrance of all kinds of delusion.

In order to remove some of the rubbish which may have accumulated in the minds of certain of our readers, and thus prepare the way for their consideration of the truth, let us briefly touch upon the negative side. First, scriptural sanctification is not a blessing which may be and often is separated from justification by a long interval of time. Those who contend for a 'second work of grace' insist that the penitent sinner is justified the moment he believes in Christ, but that he is not sanctified until he completely surrenders to the Lord and then receives the Spirit in his fullness – as though a person might be converted without fully surrendering to Christ, or become a child of God without the Holy Spirit indwelling him. This is a serious mistake. Once we are united to Christ by the Spirit and faith, we become 'joint heirs' with him, having a valid title to *all* blessing in him. There is no dividing of the Saviour: he is the holiness of his people as well as their righteousness, and when he bestows forgiveness, he also imparts heart purity.

Second, scriptural sanctification is not a protracted process by which the Christian is made meet for heaven. The same work of divine grace which delivers a soul from the wrath to come fits him for the enjoyment of eternal glory. At what point was the penitent prodigal unsuited to the Father's house? As soon as he came and confessed his sins, the best robe was placed upon him, the ring was put on his hand, his feet were shod, and the word went forth, 'Bring hither the fatted calf, and kill it; and let us eat, and be merry: for this my son was dead, and is alive again; he was lost and is found' (Luke 15:23, 24). If a gradual progressive work of the Spirit was necessary in order to fit the soul to dwell on High, then the dying thief was not qualified to enter Paradise the very day he first believed in the Lord Jesus. 'But ye are washed, but ye are sanctified, but ye are justified in the name of the Lord Jesus' (1 Cor. 6:11) – those three things cannot be separated. 'Giving thanks unto the Father, which *hath* made us meet to be partakers of the inheritance of the saints in light' (Col. 1:12).

Third, scriptural sanctification is not the eradication of the carnal nature. The doctrine of the 'Perfectionists' hardens souls in delusion, calling evil good, and allowing themselves in sin. It greatly discourages sincere souls who labour to get holiness in the right way – by faith in Christ – and leads them to think that they labour in vain, because they find themselves still sinful and far from perfect, when they have done their best to attain it. It renders meaningless many scriptural exhortations, such as Romans 6:12, 2 Corinthians 7:1, Ephesians 4:22, 2 Timothy 2:22 – 'flee also youthful lusts', shows plainly they were still present even in the godly Timothy! Were the carnal nature gone from the Christian, he would be quite unfitted for such duties as the confessing of sins (1 John 1:9), loathing himself for them (Job 40:4), praying earnestly for the pardon of them (Matt. 6:12), sorrowing over them with godly sorrow (2 Cor. 7:10), accepting the chastisement of them (Heb. 12:5-11), vindicating God for the same (Ps. 119:75), and offering him the sacrifice of a broken and a contrite heart (Ps. 51:17).

Fourth, scriptural sanctification is not something wholly objective in Christ, which is not in anywise in ourselves. In their revolt against sinless perfectionism, there have been some who have gone to an opposite extreme: Antinomians argue for a holiness in Christ which produces no radical change for the better in the Christian. This is another deceit of the devil, for a deceit it certainly is for anyone to imagine that the *only* holiness he has is in Christ. There is no such thing in reality as a perfect and inalienable standing in Christ which is divorced from heart-purity and a personal walk in righteousness. What a flesh-pleasing dogma is it, that one act of faith in the Lord Jesus secures eternal immunity from condemnation and provides a lifelong licence to wallow in sin. *My reader, a faith which does not transform character and reform conduct is worthless.* Saving faith is only proved to be genuine by bearing the blossoms of experimental godliness and the fruits of personal piety.

In our quest after the actual nature of holiness certain definite considerations need to be kept steadily before us, as guideposts along the track which we must follow. First, by noting what is holiness in God himself, for the creature's holiness – be it the angels', Christ's, or the Christian's – must conform to the divine pattern. Though there may be many degrees of holiness, there cannot be more than one kind of holiness. Second, by ascertaining what Adam had and lost, and which Christ has regained for his people. While it be blessedly true that the Christian obtains far more in the Second Man than was forfeited by the first man, yet this is a point of considerable importance. Third, by discovering the true nature of sin, for holiness is its opposite. Fourth, by remembering that sanctification is an integral and essential part of salvation itself, and not an extra. Fifth, by following up the clue given us in the threefold meaning of the term itself.

1. What is connoted by the holiness of God? In seeking an answer to this question very little help is to be obtained from the works of theologians, most of whom contented themselves *with a set of words* which expressed no distinct thing, but left matters wholly in the dark. Most of them say that God's holiness is his purity. If it be enquired, in what does this purity consist? the usual reply is, In that which is opposite to all sin, the greatest impurity. But who is the wiser by this? That, of itself, does not help us to form any positive idea of what God's purity consists of, until we are told *what* sin really *is*. But the nature of sin cannot be experimentally known until we apprehend what holiness is, for we do not fully learn what holiness is by obtaining a right idea of sin; rather must we first know what holiness is in order for a right knowledge of sin.

A number of eminent theologians have attempted to tell us what divine holiness is by saying, It is not properly a distinct attribute of God, but the beauty and glory of all his moral perfections. But we can get no concrete idea from

75

those words, until we are told what is this 'beauty and glory'. To say it is 'holiness' is to say nothing at all to the point. All that John Gill gives us for a definition of God's holiness is 'holiness is the purity and rectitude of his nature'. Nathaniel Emmons, the perfecter of the 'New England' scheme of theology, tells us: 'Holiness is a general term to express that goodness or benevolence which comprises everything that is morally amiable and excellent'. Though sound in their substance, such statements are too brief to be of much service to us in seeking to form a definite conception of the divine holiness.

The most helpful description of God's holiness which we have met with is that framed by the Puritan, Stephen Charnock: 'It is the rectitude or integrity of the divine nature, or that conformity of it in affection and action to the divine will, as to his Eternal law, whereby he works with a becomingness to his own excellency, and whereby he hath a delight and complacency in everything agreeable to his will, and an abhorrency of every-thing contrary thereto.' Here is something definite and tangible, satisfying to the mind; though perhaps it requires another feature to be added to it. Since the law is 'a transcript' of the divine mind and nature, then God's holiness must be his own harmony therewith; to which we may add, God's holiness is his ordering all things for his own glory, for he can have no higher end than that – this being his own unique excellency and prerogative.

We fully concur with Charnock in making the will of God and the law of God one and the same thing, and that his holiness lies in the conformity of his affections and actions with the same; adding, that the furtherance of his own glory being his design in the whole. Now this concept of the divine holiness – the sum of God's moral excellency – helps us to conceive what holiness is in the Christian. It is far more than a 'position' or 'standing'. It is also and chiefly a moral quality, which produces conformity to the divine will or law, and which moves its possessor to aim at the glory of God in all things. This, and nothing short of this, could meet the divine requirements; and this is the great gift which God bestows upon his people.

2. What was it that Adam had and lost? What was it which distinguished him from all the lower creatures? Not simply the possession of a soul, but that his soul had stamped upon it *the moral image* and likeness of his Maker. This it was which constituted his blessedness, which capacitated him for communion with the Lord, and which qualified him to live a happy life to his glory. And this it was which he lost at the Fall. And this it is which the last Adam restores unto his people. That is clear from a comparison of Colossians 3:10 and Ephesians 4:23: the 'new man', the product of regeneration, is '*renewed* in knowledge (in the vital and experimental knowledge of God himself: John 17:3) after the image of him that created him', that is, after the original likeness which was bestowed upon Adam; and that 'new man' is distinctly said to be 'created in righteousness and true holiness' (Eph. 4:24).

Thus, what the first Adam lost and what the last Adam secured for his people, was the 'image and likeness' of God stamped upon the heart, which 'image' consists of 'righteousness and holiness'. Hence to understand that personal and experimental holiness which the Christian is made partaker of at the new birth, we have to go back to the beginning and ascertain what was the nature or character of that moral 'uprightness' (Eccl. 7:29) with which God created man at the beginning. Holiness and righteousness was the 'nature' with which the first man was endowed; it was the very law of his being, causing him to delight in the Lord, do those things which are pleasing in his sight, and reproduce in his creature measure God's own righteousness and holiness. Here again we discover that holiness is a moral quality, which conforms its possessor to the divine law or will, and moves him to aim only at the glory of God.

3. What is sin? Ah, what man is capable of supplying an adequate answer: 'Who can understand his errors?' (Ps. 19:12). A volume might be written thereon, and still much be left unsaid. Only the One against whom it is committed can fully understand its nature or measure its enormity. And yet, from the light which God has furnished us, a partial answer at least can be gathered. For example, in 1 John 3:4 we read, 'Sin is the transgression of the law', and that such transgression is not confined to the outward act is clear from 'the *thought* of foolishness is sin' (Prov. 24:9). But what is meant by 'sin is the transgression of the law?' It means that sin is a trampling upon God's holy commandment. It is an act of defiance against the Lawgiver. The law being 'holy and just and good', it follows that any breach of it is an evil and enormity which God alone is capable of estimating.

All sin is a breach of the eternal standard of equity. But it is more than that: it reveals an inward enmity which gives rise to the outward transgression. It is the bursting forth of that pride and the self-will which resents restraint, which repudiates control, which refuses to be under authority, which resists rule. Against the righteous restraint of law, Satan opposed a false idea of 'liberty' to our first parents – 'Ye shall be as gods'. And he is still plying the same argument and employing the same bait. The Christian must meet it by asking, Is the disciple to be above his Master, the servant superior to his Lord? Christ was 'made under the law' (Gal. 4:4), and lived in perfect submission thereto, and has left us an example that we should 'follow his steps' (1 Pet. 2:21). Only by loving, fearing, and obeying the law, shall we be kept from sinning.

Sin, then, is an inward state which precedes the evil deeds. It is a state of heart which refuses to be in subjection to God. It is a casting off the divine law, and setting up self-will and self-pleasing in its stead. Now, since holiness is the opposite of sin, this helps us to determine something more of the nature of sanctification. Sanctification is that work of divine grace in the believer which brings him back into allegiance to God, regulating his affections and actions in harmony with his will, writing his law on the heart (Heb. 10:16), moving him to make God's glory his chief aim and end. That divine work is commenced at regeneration, and completed only at glorification. It may be thought that, in this section, we have contradicted what was said in an earlier paragraph. Not so; in God's light we see light. Only after the principle of holiness has been imparted to us, can we discern the real character of sin; but after it has been received, an analysis of sin helps us to determine the nature of sanctification.

4. Sanctification is an integral part of 'salvation'. As this point was dwelt upon at length in the third chapter, there is less need for us to say much upon it here. Once it be clearly perceived that God's salvation is not only a rescue from the penalty of sin, but is as well, and chiefly, deliverance from the pollution and power of sin – ultimating in complete freedom from its very presence – there will be no difficulty in seeing that sanctification occupies a central place in the process. Alas that while there are many who think of Christ dying to secure their pardon, so few today consider Christ dying in order to renew their hearts, heal their souls, bring them unto obedience to God. One is often obliged to wonder if one out of each ten professing Christians is *really* experimentally acquainted with the '*so great* salvation' (Heb. 2:3) of God!

Inasmuch as sanctification is an important branch of salvation, we have another help towards understanding its nature. Salvation is deliverance from sin, an emancipation from the bondage of Satan, a being brought into right relations with God; and sanctification is that which makes this *actual* in the believer's experience – not perfectly so in this life, but truly so, nevertheless. Hence sanctification is not only the principal *part of* salvation, but it is also the chief *means* thereto. Salvation from the power of sin consists in deliverance from the *love* of sin; and that is effected by the principle of holiness which loves purity and piety. Again, there can be no fellowship with God, no walking with him, no delighting ourselves in him, except as we tread the path of obedience (see 1 John 1:5-7); and that is only possible as the principle of holiness is operative within us.

Let us now combine these four points. What is scriptural sanctification? First, it is a moral quality in the regenerate – the same in its nature as that which belongs to the divine character – which produces harmony with God's will and causes its possessor to aim at his glory in all things. Second, it is the moral image of God – lost by the first Adam, restored by the last Adam – stamped upon the heart, which 'image' consists of righteousness and holiness. Third, it is the opposite of sin. Inasmuch as all sin is a transgression of the divine law, true sanctification brings its possessor into a conformity thereto. Fourth, it is an integral and essential part of 'salvation', being a deliverance from the power and pollution of sin, causing its possessor to love what he once hated, and to now hate what he formerly loved. Thus, it is that which experimentally fits us for fellowship with and the enjoyment of the Holy One himself.

5. The threefold signification of the term 'to sanctify'. Perhaps the simplest and surest method to pursue in seeking to arrive at a correct understanding of the nature of sanctification is to follow up the meaning of the word itself, for in Scripture the names of things are always in accurate accord

with their character. God does not tantalize us with ambiguous or meaningless expressions, but the name he gives to a thing is a properly descriptive one. So here. The word 'to sanctify' means to consecrate or set apart for a sacred use, to cleanse or purify, to adorn or beautify. Diverse as these meanings may appear, yet as we shall see they beautifully coalesce into one whole. Using this, then, as our principal key, let us see whether the threefold meaning of the term will open for us the main avenues of our subject.

Sanctification is, first of all, an act of the triune God, whereby his people are set apart for himself – for his delight, his glory, his use. To aid our understanding on this point, let it be noted that Jude 1 speaks of those who are 'sanctified by God the Father', and that this precedes their being 'preserved in Jesus Christ and called'. The reference there is to the Father choosing his people for himself out of the race which he purposed to create, separating the objects of his favour from those whom he passed by. Then in Hebrews 10:10 we read, 'we are sanctified through the offering of the body of Jesus Christ once for all'; his sacrifice has purged his people from every stain of sin, separated them from the world, consecrated them unto God, setting them before him in all the excellency of his offering. In 2 Thessalonians 2:13 we are told, 'God hath from the beginning chosen you to salvation through sanctification of the Spirit, and belief of the truth': this refers to the Spirit's quickening work by which he separates the elect from those who are dead in sin.

Sanctification is, in the second place, *a cleansing* of those who are to be devoted to God's use. This 'cleansing' is both a legal and an experimental one. As we prosecute our subject, it needs to be constantly borne in mind that sanctification or holiness is the opposite of *sin*. Now as sin involves both guilt and pollution, its remedy must meet both of those needs and counteract both of those effects. A loathsome leper would

81

no more be a fit subject for heaven than would one who was still under the curse. The double provision made by divine grace to meet the need of God's guilty and defiled people is seen in the 'blood and water' which proceeded from the pierced side of the Saviour (John 19:34). Typically, this twofold need was adumbrated of old in the tabernacle furniture: the laver to wash at was as indispensable as the altar for sacrifice. Cleansing is as urgent as forgiveness.

That one of the great ends of the death of Christ was the moral purification of his people is clear from many scriptures. 'He died for all, that they which live should not henceforth live unto themselves, but unto him which died for them, and rose again' (2 Cor. 5:15); 'Who gave himself for us, that he might redeem us from all iniquity, and purify unto himself a peculiar people, zealous of good works' (Titus 2:14); 'How much more shall the blood of Christ, who through the eternal Spirit offered himself without spot to God, purge your conscience from dead works to serve the living God' (Heb. 9:14); 'Who his own self bare our sins in his own body on the tree, that we, being dead to sins, should live unto righteousness' (1 Pet. 2:24). From these passages it is abundantly plain that the purpose of the Saviour in all that he did and suffered, was not only to deliver his people from the *penal* consequences of their sins, but also to cleanse them from the *pollution* of sin, to free them from its enslaving power, to rectify their moral nature.

It is greatly to be regretted that so many when thinking or speaking of the 'salvation' which Christ has purchased for his people, attach to it no further idea than deliverance from condemnation. They seem to forget that deliverance from *sin* – the cause of condemnation – is an equally important blessing comprehended in it. 'Assuredly it is just as necessary for fallen creatures to be freed from the pollution and moral impotency which they have contracted, as it is to be exempted from the penalties which they have incurred; so that when re-instated in the favour of God, they may at the same time be more capable of loving, serving, and enjoying him forever. And in this respect the remedy which the gospel reveals is fully suited to the exigencies of our sinful state, providing for our *complete* redemption from sin itself, as well as from the penal liabilities it has brought upon us' (Thomas Crawford on 'The Atonement'). Christ has procured sanctification for his people as well as justification.

That cleansing forms an integral element in sanctification is abundantly clear from the types. 'For if the blood of bulls and of goats, and the ashes of an heifer sprinkling the unclean, sanctifieth to the purifying of the flesh' (Heb. 9:13). The blood, the ashes, the sprinkling, were all God's merciful provision for the 'unclean' and they sanctified 'to the purifying of the flesh' – the references being to Leviticus 16:14 and Numbers 19:2, 17, 18. The antitype of this is seen in the next verse, 'How much more shall the blood of Christ, who through the eternal Spirit offered himself without spot to God, *purge your conscience* from dead works to serve the living God.' The type availed only for a temporary and ceremonial sanctification, the Antitype for a real and eternal cleansing. Other examples of the same thing are found in, 'Go unto the people, and *sanctify* them today and tomorrow, and let them *wash* their clothes' (Exod. 19:10); 'I will sanctify also both Aaron and his sons, to minister to me in the priest's office' (Exod. 29:44) – for the accomplishment of this see Exodus 40:12-15, where we find they were 'washed with water', 'anointed' with oil, and 'clothed' or adorned with their official vestments.

Now the substitutionary and sacrificial work of Christ has produced for his people a threefold 'cleansing'. The first is judicial, the sins of his people being all blotted out as though they had never existed. Both the guilt and the defilement of their iniquities are completely removed, so that the church appears before God 'as the morning, fair as the moon, clear as the sun' (Song of Sol. 6:10). The second is personal, at 'the washing of regeneration and renewing of the Holy Spirit'. The third is experimental, when faith appropriates the cleansing blood and the conscience is purged: 'purifying their hearts by faith' (Acts 15:9), 'having our hearts sprinkled from an evil conscience, and our bodies washed with pure water' (Heb. 10:22). Unlike the first two, this last, is a repeated and continuous thing: 'If we confess our sins, he is faithful and just to forgive us our sins, and to *cleanse* us from all unrighteousness' (1 John 1:9). We hope to amplify these different points considerably when we take up more definitely our sanctification by Christ.

Sanctification is, in the third place, *an adorning* or beautifying of those whom God cleanses and sets apart unto himself. This is accomplished by the Holy Spirit in his work of morally renovating the soul, whereby the believer is made inwardly holy. That which the Spirit communicates is the life of the risen Christ, which is a principle of purity, producing love to God; and love to God implies, of course, subjection to him. Thus, holiness is an inward conformity to the things which God has commanded, as the 'pattern' (or sample) corresponds to the piece from which it is taken. 'For ye know what commandments we gave you by the Lord Jesus. For *this* is the will of God, even your sanctification' (1 Thess. 4:2, 3), i.e. your sanctification consists in a conformity to his will. Sanctification causes the heart to make God its chief good, and his glory its chief end.

As *his glory* is the end God has in view in all his actions – ordering, disposing, directing every thing with this design – so conformity to him, being holy as he is holy, must consist in setting *his glory* before us as our ultimate aim. Subjective sanctification is that change wrought in the heart which produces a steady desire and purpose to please and honour God. This is not in any of us by nature, for self-love rules the unregenerate. Calamities may drive the unsanctified toward God, yet it is only for the relief of *self*. The fear of hell may stir up a man to cry unto God for mercy, but it is only that *he* may be delivered. Such actions are only the workings of mere nature – the instinct of self-preservation; there is nothing spiritual or supernatural about them. But at regeneration a man is lifted off his own bottom and put on a new foundation.

Subjective sanctification is a change or renovating of the heart so that it is conformed unto God – unto his will, unto his glory. 'The work of sanctification is a work framing and casting the heart itself into the Word of God (as metals are cast into a die or mould), so that the heart is made of the same stamp and disposition with the Word' (Thomas Goodwin). 'Ye have obeyed from the heart that form (or 'pattern') of doctrine whereto ye were delivered' (Rom. 6:17). The arts and sciences deliver unto us rules which we must conform unto, but God's miracle of grace within his people *conforms them unto* the ruling of his will, so as to be formed by them; softening their hearts so as to make them capable of receiving the impressions of his precepts. Below we quote again from the excellent remarks of Thomas Goodwin.

'The substance of his comparison comes to this, that their hearts having been first, in the inward inclinations and disposi-tions of it, framed and changed into what the Word requires, they then obeyed the same Word from the heart naturally, willingly; and the commandments were not grievous, because the heart was framed and moulded thereunto. The heart must be made good ere men can obey from the heart; and to this end he elegantly first compares the doctrine of law and gospel delivered them, unto a pattern or sampler, which having in their eye, they framed and squared their actions and doings unto it. And he secondly compares the same doctrine unto a mould or matrix, into which metal is being delivered, which have the same figure or form left on them which the mould itself had; and this is spoken in respect of their hearts.'

This mighty and marvellous change is not in the substance or faculties of the soul, but in its disposition; for a lump of metal being melted and moulded remains the same metal it was before, yet its frame and fashion is greatly altered. When the heart has been made humble and meek, it is enabled to perceive what is that good, and perfect, and acceptable will of God, and approves of it as good for him; and thus we are 'transformed by the renewing of our mind' (Rom. 12:2). As the mould and the thing moulded correspond, as the wax has on it the image by which it was impressed, so the heart which before was enmity to every commandment, now delights in the law of God after the inward man, finding an agreeableness between it and his own disposition. Only as the heart is supernaturally changed and conformed to God is it found that 'his commandments *are not* grievous' (1 John 5:3).

What has just been said above brings us back to the point reached in the preceding chapter (or more correctly, the first sections of this chapter), namely, that holiness is a moral quality, an inclination, a 'new nature', a disposition which delights itself in all that is pure, excellent, benevolent. It is the shedding abroad of God's love in the heart, for only by *love* can his holy law be 'fulfilled'. Nothing but disinterested love (the opposite of self-love) can produce cheerful obedience. And, as Romans 5:5 tells us, the love of God is shed abroad in our hearts *by the Holy Spirit*. We are sanctified by the Spirit indwelling us, he producing in and through us the fruits of holiness. And thus it is that we read, 'But know that the LORD hath set apart him that is *godly* for himself' (Ps. 4:3).

In the preceding (portion of this) chapter we asked, 'How can it be discovered whether or not we have been sanctified, unless we really know what sanctification is?' Now let it be pointed out that our sanctification by the Father and our sanctification by Christ can only be known to us by the sanctification *of the Spirit*, and that, in turn, can only be discovered by its *effects*. And this brings us to the ultimate aspect of *the nature* of our sanctification, namely, that holy walk, or course of outward conduct, which makes manifest and is the effect of our inward sanctification by the Spirit. This branch of our subject is what theologians have designated our 'practical sanctification'. Thus, we distinguish between the act and process by which the Christian is set apart unto God, the moral and spiritual state into which that setting apart brings him, and the holy living which proceeds from that state; it is the last we have now reached. As the 'setting apart' is both privative and positive – from the service of Satan, to the service of God – so holy living is separation from evil, following that which is good.

Thomas Manton, than whom none of the Puritans are more simple, succinct, and satisfying, says:

> 'Sanctification is threefold. First, *meritorious* sanctification is Christ's meriting and purchasing for his Church the inward inhabitation of the Spirit, and that grace whereby they may be sanctified: Hebrews 10:10. Second, *applicatory* sanctification is the inward renovation, of the heart of those whom Christ hath sanctified by the Spirit of regeneration, whereby a man is translated from death to life, from the state of nature to the state of grace. This is spoken of in Titus 3:5: this is the daily sanctification, which, with respect to the merit of Christ, is wrought by the Spirit and the ministry of the Word and sacraments. Third, *practical* sanctification is that by which those for whom Christ did sanctify himself, and who are renewed by the Holy Spirit, and planted into Christ by faith, do more and more sanctify and cleanse themselves from sin in thought, word and deed: (1 Pet. 1:15; 1 John 3:3).
>
> 'As to sanctify signifieth to consecrate or dedicate to God, so it signifieth both the fixed inclination or the disposition of the soul towards God as our highest lord and chief good, and accordingly a resignation of our souls to God, to live in the love of his blessed majesty and a thankful obedience to him. More distinctly (1) it implieth a bent, a tendency, or fixed inclination towards God, which is habitual sanctification.

(2) A resignation, or giving up ourselves to God, by which actual holiness is begun; a constant using ourselves to him, by which it is continued; and the continual exercise of a fervent love, by which it is increased in us more and more, till all be perfected in glory.

As to sanctify signifieth to purify and cleanse, so it signifies the purifying of the soul from the love of the world. A man is impure because, when he was made for God, he doth prefer base trifles of this world before his Master and everlasting glory: and so he is not sanctified that doth despise and disobey his Maker; he despiseth him because he preferreth the most contemptible vanity before him, and doth choose the transitory pleasure of sinning before the endless fruition of God. Now he is sanctified when his worldly love is cured, and he is brought back again to the love and obedience of God. Those that are healed of the over-love of the world are sanctified, as the inclinations of the flesh to worldly things are broken.'

'And the very God of peace sanctify you wholly; and I pray God your whole spirit and soul and body be preserved blameless unto the coming of our Lord Jesus Christ' (1 Thess. 5:23). There was probably a threefold reference in the apostle's request. First, he prayed that all the members of the Thessalonian church, the entire assembly, might be sanctified. Second, he prayed that each individual member might be sanctified entirely in his whole man, spirit and soul and body. Third, he prayed that each and all of them might be sanctified more perfectly, moved to press forward unto complete holiness. 1 Thessalonians 5:23 is almost parallel with Hebrews 13:20, 21. The apostle prayed that all the parts and faculties of the Christian might be kept under the influence of efficacious grace, in true and real conformity to God; so influenced by the Truth as to be fitted and furnished, in all cases and circumstances, for the performance of every good work. Though this be our bounden duty, yet it lies not absolutely in our own power, but is the work of God in and through us; and thus is to form the subject of earnest and constant prayer.

Two things are clearly implied in the above passage. First, that the *whole nature* of the Christian is the subject of the work of sanctification, and not merely part of it: every disposition and power of the spirit, every faculty of the soul, the body with all its members. The *body* too is 'sanctified'. It has been made a member of Christ (1 Cor. 6:15), it is the temple of the Holy Spirit (1 Cor. 6:19). As it is an integral part of the believer's person, and as its inclinations and appetites affect the soul and influence conduct, it must be brought under the control of the spirit and soul, so that 'every one of us should know how to possess his vessel in sanctification and honour' (1 Thess. 4:4), and 'as ye have yielded your members servants to uncleanness and to iniquity unto iniquity; even so now yield your members servants to righteousness unto holiness' (Rom. 6:19).

Second, that this work of divine grace *will be* carried on to completion and perfection, for the apostle immediately adds, 'Faithful is he that calleth you, who also will do it' (1 Thess. 5:24). Thus the two verses are parallel with 'Being confident of this very thing, that he which hath begun a good work in you *will perform it* until the day of Jesus Christ' (Phil. 1:6). Nothing short of every faculty and member of the Christian being devoted to God is what he is to ever aim at. But the attainment of this is only completely realized at his glorification: 'We know that, when he shall appear, we shall be like Him' (1 John 3:2) – not only inwardly but outwardly: 'Who shall change our vile body, that it may be fashioned like unto his glorious body' (Phil. 3:21).

Its Nature (Completed)

That which we have laboured to show in the previous chapters is the fact that the sanctification of the Christian is very much more than a bare setting apart of him unto God: it is also, and chiefly, a work of grace wrought in his soul. God not only *accounts* his people holy, but actually *makes* them so. The various materials and articles used in the tabernacle of old, when dedicated to God, were changed only in their *use*, but when man is dedicated to God he is changed in his *nature*, so that not only is there a vital difference between him and others, but a radical difference between him and himself (1 Cor. 6:11) – between what he was, and now is. That change of nature is a real necessity, for the man himself must be made holy before his actions can be so. Grace is planted in the heart, from whence its influence is diffused throughout all departments of his life. Internal holiness is a hatred of sin and a love of that which is good, and external holiness is the avoiding of the one and the pursuing of the other. Wherever there be a change of heart fruits will appear in the conduct.

Like 'salvation' itself – according to the use of the term in Scripture (see 2 Tim. 1:9, salvation in the past; Phil. 2:12, salvation in the present; Rom. 13:11, salvation in the future) and in the actual history of the redeemed – so sanctification must be considered under *its three tenses*. There is a very real sense in which all of God's elect have already *been* sanctified: Jude 1; Hebrews 10:10; 2 Thessalonians 2:13. There is also a very real sense in which those of God's people on earth are daily *being* sanctified: 2 Corinthians 4:16; 2 Corinthians 7:1; 1 Thessalonians 5:23. And there is also a very real sense in which the Christian's (complete) sanctification is yet *future*: Romans 8:30; Hebrews 12:23; 1 John 3:2. Unless this threefold distinction be carefully borne in mind our thoughts are bound to be confused. Objectively, our sanctification is already an accomplished fact (1 Cor. 1:2), in which one saint shares equally with another. Subjectively, our sanctification is *not* complete in this life (Phil. 3:12) and varies considerably in different Christians, though the promise of Philippians 1:6 belongs alike to all of them.

Though our sanctification be complete in all its parts, yet it is not now perfect in its degrees. As the new-born babe possesses a soul and body, endowed with all their members, yet they are undeveloped and far from a state of maturity. So it is with the Christian, who (in comparison with the life to come) remains throughout this life but a 'babe in Christ' (1 Pet. 2:2). We know but 'in part' (1 Cor. 13:12), and we are sanctified but in part, for 'there remaineth yet very much land to be possessed' (Josh. 13:1). In the most gracious there remains a double principle: the flesh and the spirit, the old man and the new man. We are a mixture and a medley during our present state. There is a conflict between operating principles (sin and grace), so that every act is mixed: there is tin mixed with our silver and dross with our gold. Our best deeds are defiled, and therefore we continue to feed upon the Lamb *with* 'bitter herbs' (Exod. 12:8).

Holiness in the heart discovers itself by godly sorrowings and godly aspirations. 'Blessed are they that mourn: for they shall be comforted' (Matt. 5:4): 'mourn' because of the swellings of pride, the workings of unbelief, the surgings of discontent; 'mourn' because of the feebleness of their faith, the coldness of their love, their lack of conformity to Christ. *There is nothing which more plainly evidences a person to be sanctified than a broken and contrite heart – grieving over that which is contrary to holiness.* Rightly did the Puritan John Owen say, 'Evangelical repentance is that which carrieth the believing soul through all his failures, infirmities, and sins. He is not able to live one day without the constant exercise of it. *It is as necessary unto the continuance of spiritual life as faith is.* It is that continual, habitual, self-abasement which arises from a sense of the majesty and holiness of God, and the consciousness of our miserable failures.' It is this which makes the real Christian so thankful for Romans 7, for he finds it corresponds exactly with his own inward experience.

The sanctified soul, then, is very far from being satisfied with the measure of experimental holiness which is yet his portion. He is painfully conscious of the feebleness of his graces, the leanness of his soul, and the defilements from his inward corruption. But, 'Blessed are they which do hunger and thirst after righteousness' (Matt. 5:6), or 'they that are hungering and thirsting' as the Greek reads, being the participle of the present tense; intimating a *present* disposition of soul. Christ pronounces 'blessed' (in contrast from those under 'the curse') they who are hungering and thirsting after his righteousness imparted as well as imputed, who thirst after the righteousness of sanctification as well as the righteousness of justification – i.e. the Spirit infusing into the soul holy principles, supernatural graces, spiritual qualities, and then strengthening and developing the same. Such has been the experiences of the saints in all ages, 'As the hart panteth after the water brooks, so panteth my soul after thee, O God. My soul thirsteth for God, for the living God: when shall I come and appear before God?' (Ps. 42:1, 2).

One of the things which prevents so many from obtaining a right view of the nature of sanctification is that scarcely any of the bestowments of the gospel are clearly defined in their minds, all being jumbled up together. While every spiritual privilege the believer enjoys is the fruit of God's electing love and the purchase of Christ's mediation, and so are all parts of one grand whole, yet it is our loss if we fail to definitely distinguish them one from the other. Reconciliation and justification, adoption and forgiveness, regeneration and sanctification, all combine to form the present portion of those whom the Father draws to the Son; nevertheless, each of these terms stands for a specific branch of that 'great salvation' to which they were appointed. It makes much for our peace of mind and joy of heart when we are able to apprehend these things severally. We shall therefore devote the remainder of this chapter unto a comparison of sanctification with other blessings of the Christian.

1. *Regeneration and sanctification*. It may appear to some who read critically our articles on 'Regeneration' and who have closely followed what has been said in our discussion of the nature of sanctification, that we have almost, if not quite, obliterated all real difference between what is wrought in us at the new birth and what God works in us at our sanctification. It is not easy to preserve a definite line of distinction between them, because they have a number of things in common; yet the leading points of contrast between them need to be considered if we are to differentiate them in our minds. We shall therefore occupy the next two or three paragraphs with an examination of this point, wherein we shall endeavour to set forth the relation of the one to the other. Perhaps it will help us the most to consider this by saying that, in one sense, the relation between regeneration and sanctification is that of the infant to the adult.

In likening the connection between regeneration and sanctification to the relation between an infant and an adult, it should be pointed out that we have in mind our practical and progressive sanctification, and not our objective and absolute sanctification. Our absolute sanctification, so far as our state before God is concerned, is simultaneous with our regeneration. The essential thing in our regeneration is the Spirit's quickening of us into newness of life; the essential thing in our sanctification is that henceforth we are an habitation of God, through the indwelling of the Spirit, and from *that* standpoint all the subsequent progressive advances in the spiritual life are but the effects, fruits, and manifestations of that initial consecration or anointing. The consecration of the tabernacle, and later of the temple, was a single act, done once and for all: after, there were many evidences of its continuance or perpetuity. But it is with the *experimental* aspect we would here treat.

At regeneration a principle of holiness is communicated to us; practical sanctification is the *exercise* of that principle in living unto God. In regeneration the Spirit imparts saving grace; in his work of sanctification, he *strengthens and develops* the same. As 'original sin' or that indwelling corruption which is in us at our natural birth, contains within it the seeds of all sin, so that grace which is imparted to us at the new birth contains within it the seeds of all spiritual graces; and as the one develops and manifests itself as we grow, so it is with the other. 'Sanctification is a constant, progressive renewing of the whole man, whereby the new creature doth daily more and more die unto sin and live unto God. Regeneration is the birth, sanctification is the growth of this babe of grace. In regeneration, the sun of holiness rises; in sanctification it keepeth its course, and shineth brighter and brighter unto the perfect day (Prov. 4:18). The former is a specifical change from nature to grace (Eph. 5:8); the latter is a gradual change from one degree of grace to another (Ps. 84:7), whereby the Christian goeth from strength to strength till he appear before God in Zion' (George Swinnock, 1660).

Thus, the foundation of sanctification is laid in regeneration, in that a holy principle is then first formed in us. That holy principle evidences itself in conversion, which is turning away from sin to holiness, from Satan to Christ, from the world to God. It continues to evidence itself under the constant work of mortification and vivification, or the practical putting off of the old man and the putting on of the new; and is completed at glorification. The great difference then between regeneration and experimental and practical sanctification is that the former is a divine *act*, done once and for all; while the latter is a divine *work* of God's grace, wherein he sustains and develops, continues and perfects the work he then began. The one is a birth, the other the growth. The making of us practically holy is the design which God has in view when he quickens us: it is the necessary means to this end, for sanctification is the *crown* of the whole process of salvation.

One of the chief defects of modern teaching on this subject has been in regarding the new birth as the summum bonum of the spiritual life of the believer. Instead of its being the goal, it is but the starting point. Instead of being the end, it is only a means to the end. Regeneration must be supplemented by sanctification, or otherwise the soul would remain at a standstill – if such a thing were possible: for it seems to be an unchanging law in every realm that where there is no progression, there must be retrogression. That spiritual growth which is so essential lies in progressive sanctification, wherein all the faculties of the soul are more and more brought under the purifying and regulating influence of the principle of holiness which is implanted at the new birth, for thus alone do we 'grow up into him in all things, which is the Head, even Christ' (Eph. 4:15).

2. *Justification and sanctification*. The relation between justification and sanctification is clearly revealed in Romans 3–8: that Epistle being the great doctrinal treatise of the New Testament. In the fifth chapter we see the believing sinner declared righteous before God and at peace with him, given an immutable standing in his favour, reconciled to him, assured of his preservation, and so rejoicing in hope of the glory of God. Yet, great as are these blessings, something more is required by the quickened conscience, namely, deliverance from the power and pollution of inherited sin. Accordingly, this is dealt with at length in Romans 6, 7, 8, where various fundamental aspects of sanctification are treated. First it is demonstrated that the believer has been *judicially* cleansed from sin and the curse of the law, and that, in order that he may be *practically* delivered from the dominion of sin, so that he may delight in and serve the law. Union with Christ not only involves identification with his death, but participation in his resurrection.

Yet though sanctification is discussed by the apostle *after* his exposition of justification, it is a serious error to conclude that there may be, and often is, a considerable interval of time between the two things, or that sanctification is a consequence of justification; still worse is the teaching of some that, having been justified we must now seek sanctification, without which we must certainly perish – thus making the security of justification to depend upon a holy walk. No, though the two truths are dealt with singly by the apostle, they are inseparable: though they are to be contemplated alone, they must not be divided. Christ cannot be halved: in him the believing sinner has both righteousness and holiness. Each department of the gospel needs to be considered distinctly, but not pitted against each other. Let us not draw a false conclusion, then, because justification is treated of in Romans 3 – 5 and sanctification in 6 – 8: the one passage supplements the other: they are two halves of one whole.

The Christian's regeneration is not the cause of his justification, nor is justification the cause of his sanctification – for *Christ* is the cause of all three; yet there is an *order* preserved between them: not an order of time, but of nature. First we are recovered to God's image, then to his favour, and then to his fellowship. So inseparable are justification and sanctification that sometimes the one is presented first and sometimes the other: see Romans 8:1 and 13; 1 John 1:9; then Micah 7:19 and 1 Corinthians 6:11. First, God quickens the dead soul: being made alive spiritually, he is now capacitated to act faith in Christ, by which he is (instrumentally) justified. In sanctification the Spirit carries on and perfects the work in regeneration, and that progressive work is accomplished under the new relation into which the believer is introduced by justification. Having been judicially reconciled to God, the way is now open for an experimental fellowship with him, and that is maintained as the Spirit carries forward his work of sanctification.

> 'Though justification and sanctification are both of them bless-ings of grace, and though they are absolutely inseparable, yet they are so manifestly distinct, that there is in various respects a wide difference between them. Justification respects the person in a legal sense, is a single act of grace, and terminates in a relative change; that is, a freedom from punishment and a right to life. Sanctification regards him in an experimental sense, is a continued work of grace, and terminates in a real change, as to the quality both of habits and actions. The former is by a righteousness without us; the latter is by holiness wrought in us. Justification is by Christ as a priest, and has regard to the guilt of sin; sanctification is by him as a king, and refers to its dominion. Justification is instantaneous and complete in all its real subjects; but sanctification is progres-sive' (A. Booth, 1813).

3. *Purification and sanctification.* These two things are not absolutely identical: though inseparable, they are yet distinguishable. We cannot do better than quote from George Smeaton, 'The two words frequently occurring in the ritual of Israel, "sanctify" and "purify", are so closely allied in sense, that some regard them as synonymous. But a slight shade of distinction between the two may be discerned as follows. It is assumed that ever-recurring defilements, of a ceremonial kind, called for sacrifices which removed, and the word "purify" referred to these rites and sacrifices which removed the stains which excluded the worshipper from the privilege of approach to the sanctuary of God, and from fellowship with his people. The defilement which he contracted excluded him from access. But when this same Israelite was purged by sacrifice, he was re-admitted to the full participation of the privilege. He was then *sanctified*, or *holy*. Thus the latter is the consequence of the former. We may affirm, then, that the two words in this reference to the old worship, are very closely allied; so much so, that the

one involves the other. This will throw light upon the use of these two expressions in the N. T.: Ephesians 5:25, 26; Hebrews 2:11; Titus 2:14. All these passages represent a man defiled by sin and excluded from God, but re-admitted to access and fellowship, and so pronounced holy, as soon as the blood of sacrifice is applied to him.' Often the term 'purge' or 'purify' (especially in Hebrews) includes justification as well.

Objective holiness is the result of a *relationship* with God, he having set apart some thing or person for his own pleasure. But the setting apart of one *unto* God necessarily involves the separating of it from all that is opposed to him: all believers were set apart or consecrated to God by the sacrifice of Christ. Subjective holiness is the result of a *work* of God wrought in the soul, setting that person apart for his use. Thus 'holiness' has two fundamental aspects. Growing out of the second is the soul's apprehension of God's claims upon him, and his presentation of himself unto God for his exclusive use (Rom. 12:1; etc.), which is *practical* sanctification. The supreme example of all three is found in Jesus Christ, the *Holy* One of God. Objectively, he was the One 'whom the Father hath sanctified, and sent into the world' (John 10:36); subjectively, he 'received the Spirit without measure' (John 3:34); and practically, he lived for the glory of God, being absolutely devoted to his will – only with this tremendous difference: *he* needed no inward purification as we do.

To sum up. Holiness, then, is both a relationship and moral quality. It has both a negative and a positive side: cleansing from impurity, adorning with the grace of the Spirit. Sanctification is, first, *a position of honour* to which God has appointed his people. Second, it is *a state of purity* which Christ has purchased for them. Third, it is *an enduement* given to them by the Holy Spirit. Fourth, it is *a course of devoted conduct* in keeping therewith. Fifth, it is a *standard of moral perfection*, at which they are ever to aim: 1 Peter 1:15. A 'saint' is one who was chosen in Christ before the foundation of the world (Eph. 1:4), who has been cleansed from the guilt and pollution of sin by the blood of Christ (Heb. 13:12), who has been consecrated to God by the indwelling Spirit (2 Cor. 1:21, 22), who has been made inwardly holy by the impartation of the principle of grace (Phil. 1:6), and whose duty, privilege, and aim is to walk suitable thereto (Eph. 4:1).

7

Its Author

God himself is the alone source and spring of all holiness. There is nothing of it in any creature but what is immediately from the Holy One. When God first created man, he made him in his own image, that is, 'in righteousness and true holiness' (Eph. 4:24 and cf. Col. 3:10). The creature can no more produce holiness of himself than he can create life: for the one he is just as much dependent upon God as he is for the other. How much less, then, can a *fallen* creature, polluted and enslaved by sin, sanctify himself? More easily could the Ethiopian change his skin or the leopard his spots, than a moral leper make himself pure. Where any measure of real holiness is found in a human heart its possessor must say with Paul, 'By the grace of God I am what I am' (1 Cor. 15:10). Sanctification, then, is the immediate work and gift of God himself.

No greater delusion can seize the minds of men than that defiled nature is able to cleanse itself, that fallen and ruined man may rectify himself, or that those who have lost the image of God which he created in them, should create it again in themselves by their own endeavours. Self-evident as is this truth, yet pride ever seeks to set it aside. Self-complacency assumes that obligation and ability are co-extensive. Not so. It is true that God requires and commands us *to be holy* for he will not relinquish his rights or lower his standard. Yet his command no more denotes that we have the power to comply, than his setting before us a perfect standard implies we are able to measure up to the same. Rather does the one inform us that we are *without* what God requires, the other should humble us into the dust because we come so far short of the glory of God.

But so self-sufficient and self-righteous are we by nature it also needs to be pointed out that, the very fact God promises to *work in his people* by his grace both indicates and demonstrates that of themselves they are quite unable to meet his demands. Ponder for a moment the following:

> 'I will put my law in their inward parts, and write it in their hearts; and will be their God, and they shall be my people' (Jer. 31:33);
>
> 'I will give them one heart, and one way, that they may fear me forever, for the good of them, and of their children after them: and I will make an everlasting covenant with them, that I will not turn away from them, to do them good; but I will put my fear in their hearts, that they shall not depart from me' (Jer. 32:39, 40);
>
> 'A new heart also will I give you, and a new spirit will I put within you: and I will take away the stony heart out of your flesh, and I will give you an heart of flesh; and I will put my Spirit within you, and cause you to walk in my statutes' (Ezek. 36:26, 27).

In those blessed assurances, and nowhere else, is contained the guarantee of our sanctification: all turns upon *God's* power, grace and operations. He is the alone accomplisher of his own promises.

The Author of our sanctification is the Triune God. We say 'the *Triune God*', because in Scripture the title 'God', when it stands unqualified, is not used with a uniform signification. Sometimes 'God' refers to the first Person in the Trinity, sometimes to the second Person, and sometimes to the Third. In other passages, like 1 Corinthians 15:28, for instance, it includes all the three Persons. Each of the Eternal Three has his own distinctive place or part in connection with the sanctification of the Church, and it is necessary for us to clearly perceive this if we are to have definite views thereof. We have now reached that stage in our prosecution of this subject where it behooves us to carefully trace out the particular operations of *each* divine Person in connection with our sanctification, for only as these are discerned by us will we be prepared to intelligently offer unto each One the praises which is his distinctive due.

In saying that the Author of sanctification is the Triune God, we do not mean that the Father is the Sanctifier of the Church in precisely the same way or manner as the Son or as the Holy Spirit is. No, rather is it our desire to emphasize the fact that the Christian is equally indebted unto each of the three divine Persons, that his sanctification proceeds as truly from the Father as it does from the Holy Spirit, and as actually from the Son as it does from either the Spirit or the Father. Many writers have failed to make this clear. Yet it needs to be pointed out that, in the economy of salvation, there is an *official order* observed and preserved by the Holy Three, wherein we are given to see that all is *from* the Father, all is *through* the Son, all is *by* the Holy Spirit. Not that this official order denotes any essential subordination or inferiority of one Person to another, but that each manifests himself distinctively, each displays his own glory, and each is due the separate adorations of his people.

It is most blessed to observe there is a beautiful *order* adopted and carried on by the Eternal Three through all the departments of divine love to the Church, so that each glorious Person of the Godhead has taken part in every act of grace manifested toward the mystical Body of Christ. Though all Three work conjointly, yet there are distinct Personal operations, by which they make way for the honour of each other: the love of the Father for the glory of the Son, and the glory of the Son for the power of the Holy Spirit. Thus it is in connection with the subject now before us. In the Scriptures we read that the Church is 'sanctified by God *the Father*' (Jude 1), and again, 'Wherefore Jesus also, that *he* might sanctify the people with his own blood, suffered without the gate' (Heb. 13:12), and yet again, 'God hath from the beginning chosen you to salvation through sanctification *of the Spirit*' (2 Thess. 2:13). Each Person of the Godhead, then, is our Sanctifier, though not in the same manner.

This same co-operation by the Holy Three is observable in many other things. It was so in the creation of the world: 'God that made the world and all things therein, seeing that he is Lord of heaven and earth' (Acts 17:24), where the reference is plainly to the Father; of the Son it is affirmed 'All things were made by him; and without him was not any thing made that was made' (John 1:3); while in Job 26:13 we are told, 'By his Spirit he hath garnished the heavens'. So with the production of the sacred humanity of our Redeemer: the supernatural impregnation of the Virgin was the immediate effect of the Spirit's agency (Luke 1:35), yet the human nature was voluntarily and actively assumed by Christ himself: 'he took upon him the form of a servant' (Phil. 2:7 and cf. 'took part' in Heb. 2:14); while in Hebrews 10:5 we hear the Son saying to the Father, 'a body hast *thou* prepared me'.

Our present existence is derived from the joint operation of the divine agency of the blessed Three: 'Have we not all one Father? hath not one God created us?' (Mal. 2:10); of the Son it is said, 'For by him were all things created, that are in heaven, and that are in earth' (Col. 1:16); while in Job 33:4 we read, 'The Spirit of God hath made me, and the Breath of the Almighty hath given me life'. In like manner, the 'eternal life' of believers is indiscriminately ascribed to each of the divine persons: in Romans 6:23 it is attributed to the bounty of the Father, 1 John 5:11 expressly assures us that it 'is in the Son', while in Galatians 6:8 we read, 'he that soweth to the Spirit shall *of the Spirit* reap life everlasting'. By the Father we are justified (Rom. 8:33), by Christ we are justified (Isa. 53:11), by the Spirit we are justified (1 Cor. 6:11). By the Father we are preserved (1 Pet. 1:5), by the Son we are preserved (John 10:28), by the Spirit we are preserved (Eph. 4:30). By the Father we shall be raised (2 Cor. 1:9), by the Son (John 5:28), by the Spirit (Rom. 8:11).

The actions of the Persons in the Godhead are not unlike to the beautiful colours of the rainbow: those colours are perfectly blended together in one, yet each is quite distinct. So it is in connection with the several operations of the Holy Three concerning our sanctification. While it be blessedly true that the Triune God is the Author of this wondrous work, yet, if we are to observe the *distinctions* which the Holy Scriptures make in the unfolding of this theme, they require us to recognize that, in the economy of salvation, *God the Father* is, in a special manner, *the Originator* of this unspeakable blessing. In connection with the whole scheme of redemption God the Father is to be viewed as the Fountain of grace: all spiritual blessings originating in *his* goodness, and are bestowed according to the good pleasure of his sovereign will. This is clear from Ephesians 1:3: 'Blessed be the God and Father of our Lord Jesus Christ, who hath blessed us with all spiritual blessings in the heavenlies in Christ.'

That the Father is the Sanctifier of the Church is obvious from 1 Thessalonians 5:23, 'And the very God of peace sanctify you wholly; and I pray God your whole spirit and soul and body be preserved blameless unto the coming of our Lord Jesus Christ.' Here he is acknowledged as such, by prayer being made to him for the perfecting of this gift and grace. So again in Hebrews 13:20, 21, we find the apostle addressing him as follows, 'Now the God of peace, that brought again from the dead our Lord Jesus, that great Shepherd of the sheep, through the blood of the everlasting covenant, make you perfect in every good work to do his will, working in you that which is well pleasing in his sight, through Jesus Christ.' It is the furthering of this work within his people for which the apostle supplicates God. In both passages it is the Father who is sought unto. 'By the which will we are sanctified, through the offering of the body of Jesus Christ once for all' (Heb. 10:10): here the sanctification of the Church is traced back to the sovereign will of God as the supreme originating cause thereof, the reference again being to the eternal gracious purpose of the Father, which Christ came here to accomplish.

Further proof that the first Person in the divine Trinity is the immediate Author of our sanctification is found in Jude 1: 'To them that are sanctified by God the Father, and preserved in Jesus Christ and, called.' Note it is not simply 'them that are sanctified by God', but more specifically 'By God *the Father*'. Before attempting to give the meaning of this remarkable text, it needs to be pointed out that it is closely connected with those words of Christ in John 10:36, 'Say ye of him, whom the Father hath sanctified, and sent into the world, Thou blasphemest; because I said, I am the Son of God?' Our Lord was there referring to himself not as the second Person of the Godhead absolutely considered, but as the God-man Mediator, for only as such was he 'sent' by the Father. His being 'sanctified' *before* he was 'sent', has reference to a transaction in heaven ere he became incarnate. Before the foundation of the world the Father set apart Christ and ordained that he should be both the Head and Saviour of his Church, and that he should be plenteously endowed by the Spirit for his vast undertaking.

Reverting to Jude 1, we would note particularly *the order* of its statements: the 'sanctified by God the Father' *comes before* 'preserved in Jesus Christ, called'. This initial aspect of our sanctification antedates our regeneration or effectual call from darkness to light, and therefore takes us back to the eternal counsels of God. There are three things in our verse: taking them in their inverse order, there is first, our 'calling', when we were brought from death unto life; that was preceded by our being 'preserved in Jesus Christ', i.e., preserved from physical death in the womb, in the days of our infancy, during the recklessness of youth; and that also preceded by our being 'sanctified' by the Father, that is, our names being enrolled in the Lamb's book of life, we are given to Christ to be loved by him with an everlasting love and made joint-heirs with him forever and ever.

Our sanctification by the Father was *his eternal election of us*, with all that that term connotes and involves. Election was far more than a bare choice of persons. It included our being predestined unto the adoption of children by Jesus Christ to himself (Eph. 1:5). It included our being made 'vessels unto honour' and being 'afore prepared to glory' (Rom. 9:21, 23). It included being 'appointed to obtain salvation by our Lord Jesus Christ' (1 Thess. 5:9). It included our being separated for God's pleasure, God's use, and 'that we should be to the praise of his glory' (Eph. 1:12). It included our being made 'holy and without blame before him' (Eph. 1:4). This eternal sanctification by God the Father is also mentioned in 2 Timothy 1:9: 'Who hath saved us, and called us with *an holy calling*, not according to our works, but according to his own purpose and grace, which was given us in Christ Jesus *before the world began*'.

As we pointed out in the last paragraph of the preceding chapter, 'Sanctification is, first, *a position of honour* to which God hath appointed his people'. That position of honour was their being 'chosen *in Christ* before the foundation of the world' (Eph. 1:4), when they were constituted members of his mystical Body by the eternal purpose of God. O what an amazing honour was that! a place in glory higher than that of the angels being granted them. Our poor minds are staggered before such wondrous grace. Here, then, is the link of connection between John 10:36 and Jude 1: Christ was not alone in the mind of the Father when he 'sanctified' him: by the divine decree, Christ was separated and consecrated as the Head of a sanctified people. In the sanctification of Christ, all who are 'called saints' were, in him, eternally set apart, to be partakers of his own holy standing before the Father! This was an act of pure sovereignty on the Father's part.

As it is not possible that anything can add to God's *essential* blessedness (Job 22:2, 3; 35:7), so nothing whatever outside of God can possibly be a motive unto him for any of his actions. If he be pleased to bring creatures into existence, his own supreme and sovereign will must be the sole cause, as his own *manifestative* glory is his ultimate end and design. This is plainly asserted in the Scriptures: 'The Lord hath made all things for himself: yea, even the wicked for the day of evil' (Prov. 16:4), 'Thou hast created all things, and for thy pleasure they are and were created' (Rev. 4:11), 'Who hath first given to him, and it shall be recompensed unto him again? For of him, and through him, and to him, are all things: to whom be glory forever. Amen' (Rom. 11:35, 36). So it is in the ordaining of some of his creatures unto honour and glory, and appointing them to salvation in bringing them to that glory: nought but God's sovereign will was the cause, nought but his own manifestative glory is the end.

As we have shown in previous chapters, to 'sanctify' signifies to consecrate or set apart for a sacred use, to cleanse or purify, to adorn or beautify. Which of these meanings has the term in Jude 1? We believe the words 'sanctified by God the Father' include all three of those definitions. First, in that eternal purpose of his, the elect were *separated* from all other creatures, and predestinated unto the adoption of sons. Second, in God's foreviews of his elect falling in Adam, the corrupting of their natures, and the defilement which their personal acts of sin would entail, he ordained that the Mediator should make a full atonement for them, and by his blood *cleanse* them from all sin. Third, by choosing them in Christ, the elect were united to him and so made one with him that all *his* worthiness and perfection becomes theirs too; and thus they were *adorned*. God never views them apart from Christ.

'To the praise of the glory of his grace, wherein he hath made us accepted in the Beloved' (Eph. 1:6). The Greek word for 'accepted' is 'charitoo', and Young's Concordance gives as its meaning 'to make gracious'. It occurs (as a passive participle, rather than in its active form, as in Eph. 1:6) again only in Luke 1:28, where the angel said to the Virgin, 'Hail, *highly favoured* one', which Young defines as 'to give grace, to treat graciously', and in his Index 'graciously accepted or much graced'. This, we believe, is the exact force of it in Ephesians 1:6: 'according as he hath *much graced* us in the Beloved'. A careful reading of the immediate context will show that this was *before* the foundation of the world, which is confirmed by the fact that the elect's being 'much graced in the Beloved' comes *before* 'redemption' and 'forgiveness of sins' in v. 7! – note too the 'hath' in vv. 3, 4, 6 and the change to 'have' in v. 7!

Here, then, is the ultimate reference in '*sanctified* by God the Father' (Jude 1). As we have so often pointed out in the previous chapters 'sanctification' is not a bare act of simply setting apart, but involves or includes the adorning and beautifying of the object or person thus set apart, so *fitting it for* God's use. Thus it was in God's eternal purpose. He not only made an election from the mass of creatures to be created; he not only separated those elect ones from the others, but he chose them 'in Christ', and 'much graced them in the Beloved!' The elect were made the mystical

Body and Bride of Christ, so united to him that whatever grace Christ hath, by virtue of their union with him, his people have: and therefore did he declare, 'Thou hast loved *them* AS thou loved *me*' (John 17:23). O that it may please the Holy Spirit to so shine upon our feeble understandings that we may be enabled to lay hold of this wondrous, glorious, and transcendent fact. 'Sanctified by God the Father': set apart by him to be Body and Bride of Christ, 'much graced' in him, possessing his own holy standing before the throne of heaven.

8

Its Procurer

We have now reached what is to our mind the most important and certainly the most blessed aspect of our many-sided subject, yet that which is the least understood in not a few circles of Christendom. It is the *objective* side of sanctification that we now turn to, that perfect and unforfeitable holiness which every believer has in Christ. We are *not* now going to write upon sanctification as a moral quality or attribute, nor of that which is a matter of experience or attainment by us; rather shall we contemplate something entirely *outside ourselves*, namely, that which is a fundamental part of our standing and state in Christ. That which we are about to consider is one of those 'spiritual blessings' which God has blest us with 'in the heavenlies in Christ' (Eph. 1:3). It is an immediate consequence of his blood-shedding, and results from our actual union with him as 'the Holy One of God'. It is that which his perfect offering has sanctified us *unto*, as well as what it has sanctified us *from*.

Among all the terrible effects and fruits which sin produces, the two chief are alienation from God and condemnation by God: sin necessarily excludes from his sanctuary, and brings the sinner before the judgment seat of his law. Contrariwise, among all the blessed fruits and effects which Christ's sacrifice procures, the two chief ones

111

are justification and sanctification: it cannot be otherwise. Inasmuch as Christ's sacrifice has 'put away' (Heb. 9:26), 'made an end' (Dan. 9:24) of the sins of his people, they are not only freed from all condemnation, but they are also given the right and the meetness to draw nigh unto God as purged worshippers. Sin not only entails guilt, it *defiles*; and the blood of Christ has not only secured pardon, it cleanses. Yet simple, clear, and conclusive as is this dual fact, Christians find it much harder to apprehend the second part of it than they do the first.

When we first believed in Christ, and 'the burden of our sins rolled away', we supposed that (as one hymn expresses it) we would be 'happy all the day'. Assured of God's forgiveness, that we had entered his family by the new birth, and that an eternity with Christ in unclouded bliss was our certain inheritance, what could possibly dampen our joy? Ah, but it was not long before we discovered that we were still *sinners*, living in a world of sin: yea, as time went on, we were made more and more conscious of the sink of iniquity that indwells us, ever sending forth its foul streams, polluting our thoughts, words and actions. This forced from us the agonized inquiry, *How* can such vile creatures as we see, feel, and know ourselves to be, either pray to, serve, or worship the thrice holy God? Only in his own blessed Word can be found a sufficient and a satisfying answer to this burning question.

'The epistle to the Romans is, as is well known, that part of Scripture in which the question of justification is most fully treated. There, especially, we are taught to think of God as a Judge presiding in the courts of his holy judgment. Accordingly, the expressions employed throughout that epistle are "forensic", or "judicial". They refer to our relation to God, or his relation to us, in his judicial courts – the great question there being, how criminals can be brought into such a relation to him, as to have, not criminality, but righteousness, imputed to them.

'But if, in the epistle to the Romans, we see God in the courts of his judgment, equally in the epistle to the Hebrews we see him in the temple of his worship. "Sanctified" is a word that has the same prominence in the epistle to the Hebrews that "justified" has in the epistle to the Romans. It is a *temple*-word, descriptive of our relation to God in the courts of his worship, just as 'justified' is a *forensic* word, descriptive of our relation to God in the Courts of his judgment. Before there can be any question about serving or worshipping God acceptably, the necessity of his holiness requires that the claims both of the courts of his judgment, and also of the courts of his worship, should be fully met. He who is regarded in the judicial courts of God as an unpardoned criminal, or who, in relation to the temple of God, is regarded as having the stains of his guilt upon him, cannot be allowed to take his stand among God's servants. No leper that was not thoroughly cleansed could serve in the tabernacle. The existence of one stain not adequately covered by compensatory atonement, shuts out from the presence of God.

'We must stand "unchanged" in relation to the judicial courts of God and imputatively "spotless" in relation to the courts of his worship: in other words, we must be perfectly "justified" and perfectly "sanctified" before we can attempt to worship or serve him. "Sanctification" therefore, when used in this sense, is not to be contrasted with justification, as if the latter were complete, but the former incomplete and progressive. *Both are complete to the believer*. The same moment that brings the complete "justification" of the fifth of Romans, brings the equally complete "sanctification" of the tenth of Hebrews – both being equally needed in order that God, as respects the claims of his holiness, might be "appeased" or "placated" toward us; and therefore equally needed as prerequisites to our entrance on the worship and service of God in his heavenly temple: for until wrath is effectually appeased there can be no entrance into heaven.

'The complete and finished sanctification of believers by the blood of Jesus, is the great subject of the ninth and tenth of the Hebrews. "The blood of bulls and goats" gave to them who were sprinkled therewith a title to enter into the courts of the typical tabernacle, but that title was not an abiding title. It was no sooner gained than it was lost by the first recurring taint. Repetition therefore of offering and repetition of

> sprinkling was needed again and again. The same circle was
> endlessly trodden and retrodden; and yet never was perpe-
> tuity of acceptance obtained. The tabernacle and its services
> were but shadows; but they teach us that, as "the blood of
> bulls and goats" gave to them who were sprinkled therewith
> a temporary title to enter into that typical tabernacle; so, the
> blood of Christ, once offered, gives to all those who are once
> sprinkled therewith (and all believers *are* sprinkled) a title, not
> temporary, but abiding, to enter into God's presence as those
> who are sanctified for heaven' (B. W. Newton).

'We are sanctified through the offering of the body of Jesus
Christ once for all .... For by one offering he hath *perfected
forever* them that are sanctified' (Heb. 10:10, 14). These
blessed declarations have no reference whatsoever to
anything which the Spirit does in the Christian, but relate
exclusively to what Christ has secured *for* them. They speak
of that which results from our *identification* with Christ.
They affirm that by virtue of the sacrifice of Calvary every
believer is not only counted righteous in the courts of God's
judgment, but is perfectly hallowed for the courts of his
worship. The precious blood of the Lamb not only delivers
from hell, but it also fits us for heaven.

By the redemptive work of Christ the entire Church has
been set apart, consecrated unto and accepted by God.
The grand truth is that the feeblest and most uninstructed
believer was as *completely sanctified before God* the first
moment that he trusted in Christ, as he will be when he
dwells in heaven in his glorified state. True, both his sphere
and his circumstances will then be quite different from what
they now are: nevertheless, his title to heaven, his meetness
for the immediate presence of the thrice Holy One, will be
no better then that it is today. It is *his relation to Christ* (and
that alone) which qualifies him to enter the Father's House;
and it is his relation to Christ (and that alone) which gives
him the right to *now* draw nigh within the veil. True, the
believer still carries around with him 'this body of death' (a

depraved nature), but that *affects not* his perfect standing, his completeness in Christ, his acceptance, his justification and sanctification before God. But as we said in an earlier paragraph, the Christian finds it much easier to believe in or grasp the truth of justification, than he does of his present perfect sanctification in Christ. For this reason we deem it advisable to proceed slowly and enter rather fully into this aspect of our subject. Let us begin with our Lord's own words in John 17:19: 'For their sakes I sanctify myself, that they also might be sanctified through the truth.' Unto what did Christ allude when he there spoke of sanctifying himself? Certainly he could not possibly be referring to anything subjective or experimental, for in his own person he was 'the Holy One of God', and as such, he could not increase in holiness, or become more holy. His language then must have respect unto what was *objective*, relating to the exercise of his mediatorial office.

When Christ said, 'For their sakes I sanctify myself', he denoted that he was then on the very point of dedicating himself to the full and final execution of the work of making himself a sacrifice for sin, to satisfy all the demands of God's law and justice. Christ, then, was therein expressing his readiness to present himself before the Father as the Surety of his People, to place himself on the altar as a vicarious propitiation for his Church. It was 'for the sake' of others that he sanctified himself: for the sake of his eleven apostles, who are there to be regarded as the representatives of the entire Election of Grace, It is on their behalf, for their express benefit, that he set himself apart unto the full discharge of his mediatorial office, that the fruit thereof might redound unto them. Christ unreservedly devoted himself unto God, that his people might reap the full advantages thereof.

The particular end here mentioned of Christ's sanctifying himself was 'that they also might be *sanctified* through the truth', which is a very faulty rendering of the original, the Greek preposition being 'in' and not 'through', and there is no article before 'truth'. The marginal rendering therefore, is much to be preferred: 'that they might be truly sanctified' – Bagster's interlinear and the Revised Version give 'sanctified in truth'. The meaning is 'that they might be' actually, really, verily 'sanctified' – in contrast from the typical and ceremonial sanctification which obtained under the Mosaic dispensation: compare John 4:24; Colossians 1:6, 1 John 3:18 for 'in truth'. As the result of Christ's sanctifying himself – devoting himself as a whole burnt offering to God, his people are perfectly sanctified: their sins are put away, their persons are cleansed from all defilement; and not only so, but the excellency of his infinitely meritorious work is imputed to them, so that they are perfectly acceptable to God, meet for his presence, fitted for his worship.

'For by one offering he hath perfected forever them that are sanctified' (Heb. 10:14) – not by anything which the Spirit works in them, but solely by what Christ's sanctifying of himself has wrought for them. It is this sanctification and through Christ which gives Christians their *priestly* character, the title to draw near unto God within the veil as purged worshippers. Access to God, or the worship of a people made nigh by blood, was central in the Divinely appointed system of Judaism (Heb. 9:13). The antitype, the substance, the blessed reality of this, is what Christ has secured for his Church. Believers are already perfectly sanctified *objectively*, as the immediate fruit of the Saviour's sacrifice. Priestly nearness is now their blessed portion in consequence of Christ's priestly offering of himself. This it is, and nought else, which gives us 'boldness to enter into the Holiest' (Heb. 10:19).

Many Christians who are quite clear that they must look alone to *Christ* for their justification before God, often fail to view *him* as their complete sanctification before God. But this ought not to be, for Scripture is just as clear on the one point as on the other; yea the two are therein inseparably joined together. 'But of him are ye in Christ Jesus, who of God is made unto us wisdom, and righteousness, and sanctification, and redemption' (1 Cor. 1:30). And here we must dissent from the exposition of this verse given by Charles Hodge (in his commentary) and others of his school, who interpret 'sanctification' here as Christ's Spirit indwelling his people as the Spirit of holiness, transforming them unto his likeness. But this verse is speaking of that sanctification which *Christ is made unto us*, and not that which we are *made by Christ* – the distinction is real and vital, and to ignore or confound it is inexcusable in a theologian.

Christ crucified (see the context of 1 Cor. 1:30 – vv. 17, 18, 23), 'of God is made unto us' four things, and this is precisely the same way that God 'made him (Christ) to be sin for us' (2 Cor. 5:21), namely, objectively and imputatively. First, Christ is 'made unto us wisdom', objectively, for he is the One in whom all the treasures of wisdom and knowledge are hid. It is true that by the Spirit we are made wise unto salvation, nevertheless, we are far from being as wise as we ought to be – see 1 Corinthians 8:2. But all the wisdom God requires of us is found in Christ, and as the 'Wisdom' of the book of Proverbs, he is ours. Second, Christ is 'made unto us righteousness', objectively, as he is himself 'The Lord our righteousness' (Jer. 23:6), and therefore does the believer exclaim, 'In the LORD have I righteousness and strength' (Isa. 45:24). As the law raises its accusing voice against me, I point to Christ as the One who has, by his active and passive obedience, met its every demand on my behalf.

Third, Christ is 'made unto us sanctification', *objectively*: in him we have an absolute purity, and by the imputation to us of the efficacy and merits of his cross-work we who were excluded from God on account of sin, are now given access to him. If Israel became a holy people when sprinkled with the blood of bulls and goats, so that they were readmitted to Jehovah's worship, how much more has the infinitely valuable blood of Christ sanctified us, so that we may approach God as acceptable worshippers. This sanctification is not something which we have in our own persons, but was ours in Christ as soon as we laid hold of him by faith. Fourth, Christ is 'made unto us redemption' *objectively*: he is in his own person both our redeemer and redemption – '*in whom* we have redemption' (Eph. 1:7). Christ is 'made unto us redemption' not by enabling us to redeem ourselves, but by himself paying the price.

1 Corinthians 1:30, then, affirms that we are *complete* in Christ: that whatever the law demands of us, it has received on our account in the Surety. If we are considered as what we are in ourselves, not as we stand in Christ (as one with him), then a thousand things may be 'laid to our charge'. It may be laid to our charge that we are woefully ignorant of many parts of the divine will: but the sufficient answer is, Christ is our wisdom. It may be laid to our charge that all our righteousnesses are as filthy rags: but the sufficient answer is, that Christ is our righteousness. It may be laid to our charge that we do many things and fail to do many others which unfit us for the presence of a holy God: but the sufficient answer is, that Christ is our sanctification. It may be laid to our charge that we are largely in bondage to the flesh: but the sufficient answer is, Christ is our redemption.

1 Corinthians 1:30, then, is *a unit*: we cannot define the 'wisdom' and the 'sanctification' as what the Spirit works in us, and the 'righteousness' and the 'redemption' as what Christ has wrought for us: all four are either objective or subjective. Christ is here said to be 'sanctification' unto us, just as he is our righteousness and redemption. To suppose that the sanctification here spoken of is that which is wrought in us, would oblige me to explain the righteousness

nd redemption here spoken of, as that which we had in ourselves; but such a thought Mr Hodge would rightly have ejected with abhorrence. The righteousness which Christ is 'made unto us' is most certainly not the righteousness which he works in us (the Romanist heresy), but the righteousness which he wrought out *for* us. So it is with the sanctification which Christ is 'made unto us': it is not in ourselves, but in him; it is not an incomplete and progressive thing, but a perfect and eternal one.

God has made Christ to be sanctification unto us by imputing to us the infinite purity and excellency of his sacrifice. We are made nigh to God by Christ's blood (Eph. 2:13) *before* we are brought nigh to him by the effectual call of the Spirit (1 Pet. 2:9): the former being the necessary foundation of the latter – in the types the oil could only be placed upon the blood. And it is on this account we 'are sanctified in Christ Jesus, called saints' (1 Cor. 1:2). How vastly different is this – how immeasurably superior to what the advocates of 'the higher life' or of the 'victorious life' set before their hearers and readers! It is not merely that Christ is able to do this or willing to do that for us, but every Christian *is already* 'sanctified in Christ Jesus'. My ignorance of this does not alter the blessed fact, and neither does my failure to clearly understand nor the weakness of my faith to firmly grasp it, in anywise impair it. Nor have my feelings or experience anything whatever to do with it: God says it, God *has* done it, and nothing can alter it.

Its Procurer (2)

It has been pointed out in the earlier chapters of this book that the Scriptures present the believer's sanctification from several distinct points of view: the chief of which are, first, our sanctification in the eternal purpose of God, when in his decree he chose us in Christ 'that we should be *holy* and without blame before Him' (Eph. 1:4). That is what is referred to at the beginning of Hebrews 10:10, 'by the which *will* we are sanctified'. This is our sanctification by God the Father (Jude 1), which was considered by us in the eleventh chapter under 'the Author of our Sanctification'. Second, there is the *fulfilling* of that 'will' of God, the accomplishing of his eternal purpose by our actual sanctification through the sacrifice of Christ. That is what is referred to in 'Wherefore Jesus also, that he might sanctify the people with his own blood, suffered without the gate' (Heb. 13:12). This is our sanctification by God the Son, and is what we are now considering. Third, there is the *application* of this sanctification to the individual by the Holy Spirit, when he separates him from those who are dead in sins by quickening him, and by the new birth imparting to him a new nature. This is our sanctification by God the Spirit.

Fourth, there is the *fruit* of these in the Christian's character and conduct whereby he is separated in his life and walk from the world which lieth in the wicked one, and this is by the Holy Spirit's working in him and applying the Word to him, so that he is (in measure – for now we see 'through a glass darkly') enabled to apprehend by faith his separation to God by the precious blood of Christ. Yet both his inward and outward life is far from being perfect, for though possessing a new and spiritual nature, the flesh remains in him, unchanged, to the end of his earthly pilgrimage. Those around him know little or nothing of the inward conflict of which he is the subject: they see his outward failures, but hear not his secret groanings before God. It is not yet made manifest what he shall be, but though very imperfect at present through indwelling sin, yet the promise is sure 'when he shall appear *we shall be like him, for we shall see him as he is*'.

Now though in this fourth sense our *practical* sanctification is incomplete, this in no wise alters the fact, nor to the lightest degree invalidates it, that our sanctification in the first three senses mentioned above is entire and eternal, that 'by one offering Christ hath perfected forever them that are sanctified' (Heb. 10:14). Though these three phases of the believer's sanctification are quite distinct as to their development or manifestation, yet they are blessedly combined together, and form our one complete acceptance before God. That which we are here considering has to do with the *objective* side of our subject: by which we mean that it is something entirely *outside of ourselves*, resulting from what Christ has done for us. It is that which we have in Christ and by Christ, and therefore it can be received and enjoyed by *faith alone*. O what a difference it makes to the peace and joy of the soul once the child of God firmly grasps the blessed truth that a perfect sanctification is his present and inalienable portion, that God has made Christ to be unto him sanctification as well as righteousness.

Every real Christian has already been sanctified or set apart *as holy unto God* by the precious blood of the Lamb. But though many believers are consciously and confessedly *justified* by his blood' (Rom. 5:9), yet not a few of them are unwittingly dishonouring that blood by striving (in their desires after holiness of life) to *offer* God 'entire consecration' or 'full surrender' (as they call it) in order to get sanctified – so much 'living sacrifice' they present to God for so much sanctification. They have been beguiled into the attempt to lay *self* on some imaginary 'altar' so that their sinful nature might be 'consumed by the fire of the Spirit'. Alas, they neither enter into *God's* estimate of Christ's blood, nor will they accept the fact that 'the heart is deceitful above all things, and *desperately* wicked' (Jer. 17:9). They neither realize that God has 'made Christ to be sanctification unto them' nor that the carnal mind is enmity against God' (Rom. 8:7).

It is greatly to be regretted that many theologians have confined their views far too exclusively to the *legal* aspect of the atonement, whereas both the Old Testament types and the New Testament testimony, with equal clearness, exhibit its efficacy in *all* our relations to God. Because we are in Christ, *all* that he is for us must be ours. 'The blood of Christ cleanses us from *all sin*, and the believer does not more truly take his place in Christ before the justice of God as one against whom there is *no charge*, than he takes his place in Christ before the holiness of God as one upon whom there is *no stain*' (James Inglis in *Way-marks in the wilderness*, to whom we are indebted for much in this and the preceding chapter). Not only is the believer '*justified* by his blood' (Rom. 5:9), but we are '*sanctified* (set apart, consecrated unto God, fitted and adorned for his presence) through the offering of the body of Jesus Christ once for all' (Heb. 10:10). It is *this* blessed aspect of sanctification which the denominational creeds and the writings of the Puritans almost totally ignored.

In the Larger Catechism of the Westminster Assembly, the question is asked, 'What is sanctification?' To which the following answer is returned:

> 'Sanctification is a work of God's grace, whereby, they whom God hath before the foundation of the world chosen to be holy, are in time through the powerful operation of his Spirit, applying the death and resurrection of Christ unto them, renewed in their whole man after the image of God; having the seeds of repentance unto life and all other saving graces, put into their hearts, and those graces so stirred up, increased, and strengthened, as that they more and more die unto sin and rise unto newness of life.'

Now far be it from us to sit in judgment upon such an excellent and helpful production as this Catechism, which God has richly blest to thousands of his people, or that we should make any harsh criticisms against men whose shoes we are certainly not worthy to unloose. Nevertheless, we are assured that were its compilers on earth today, they would be the last of all to lay claim to any infallibility, nor do we believe they would offer any objection against their statements being brought to the bar of Holy Scripture. The best of men are but men at the best, and therefore we must call no man 'Father'. A deep veneration for servants of God and a high regard for their spiritual learning must not deter us from complying with '*Prove all things*: hold fast that which is good' (1 Thess. 5:21). The Bereans were commended for testing the teachings even of the apostle Paul, 'And searched the Scriptures daily *whether* those things were so' (Acts 17:11). It is in this spirit that we beg to offer two observations on the above quotation.

First, the definition or description of sanctification of the Westminster divines is altogether *inadequate*, for it entirely omits the most important aspect and fundamental element in the believer's sanctification: it says nothing about our sanctification *by Christ* (Heb. 10:10; 13:12), but confines itself to the work of the Spirit, which is founded upon that of the Son. This is truly a serious loss, and affords another illustration that God has not granted light on *all* his Word to any one man or body of men. A fuller and better answer to the question of, 'What is sanctification?' would be, 'Sanctification is, first, that act of God whereby he set the elect apart in Christ before the foundation of the world that they should be holy. Second, it is that perfect holiness which the Church has in Christ and that excellent purity which she has before God by virtue of Christ's cleansing blood. Third, it is that work of God's Spirit which, by his quickening operation, sets them apart from those who are dead in sins, conveying to them a holy life or nature, etc.'

Thus we cannot but regard this particular definition of the Larger Catechism as being defective, for it commences at the middle, instead of starting at the beginning. Instead of placing before the believer that complete and perfect sanctification which God has made Christ to be unto him, it occupies him with the incomplete and progressive work of the Spirit. Instead of moving the Christian to look away from himself with all his sinful failures, unto Christ in whom he is 'complete' (Col. 2:10), it encouraged him to look within, where he will often search in vain for the fine gold of the new creation amid all the dross and mire of the old creation. This is to leave him without the joyous assurance of knowing that he has been 'perfected forever' by the one offering of Christ (Heb. 10:14); and if he be destitute of that, then doubts and fears must constantly assail him, and the full assurance of faith elude every striving after it.

Our second observation upon this definition is, that its wording is faulty and misleading. Let the young believer be credibly assured that he will 'more and more die unto sin and rise unto newness of life', and what will be the inevitable outcome? As he proceeds on his way, the devil assaulting him more and more fiercely, the inward conflict between the flesh and the Spirit becoming more and more distressing, increasing light from God's Word more and more exposing his sinful failures, until the cry is forced from him, 'I am vile; O wretched man that I am', what conclusion *must* he draw? Why this: if the Catechism-definition be correct then I was sadly mistaken, *I have never been sanctified at all*. So far from the 'more and more die unto sin' agreeing with *his* experience, he discovers that sin is more active within and that he is more alive to sin now, than he was ten years ago!

Will any venture to gainsay what we have just pointed out above, then we would ask the most mature and godly reader, Dare you solemnly affirm, as in the presence of God, that *you* have 'more and more died unto sin'? If you answer, Yes, the writer for one would not believe you. But we do not believe for a moment that you would utter such an untruth. Rather do we think we can hear you saying, 'Such has been my deep *desire*, such has been my sincere design in using the means of grace, such is still my daily prayer; but alas, alas! I find as truly and as frequently today as I ever did in the past that, 'When I would do good, evil is present with me; for what I would, that do I not; but what I hate, that do I' (Rom. 7). Ah, there is a vast difference between what *ought* to be, and that which actually *obtains* in our experience.

That we may not be charged with partiality, we quote from the 'Confession of Faith' adopted by the Baptist Association, which met in Philadelphia 1742, giving the first two sections of their brief chapter on sanctification:

> 1. 'They who are united to Christ, effectually called, and regenerated, having a new heart and a new spirit in them through the virtue of Christ's death and resurrection, are also (a) farther sanctified, really and personally, through the same virtue, (b) by his Word and Spirit dwelling in them; (c) the dominion of the whole body of sin is destroyed, (d) and the several lusts thereof *more and more weakened* and mortified, and they more and more quickened and strengthened in all saving graces, to the practice of all true holiness, without which no man shall see the Lord.
>
> 2. This sanctification is throughout in the whole man, yet imperfect in this life; there abideth still *some remnants* of corruption in every part, whence ariseth a continual and irreconcilable war.' (*Italics ours*)

Like the previous one, this description of sanctification by the Baptists leaves something to be desired, for it makes no clear and direct statement upon the all-important and flawless holiness which every believer has *in Christ*, and that spotless and impeccable purity which is *upon* him by God's imputation of the cleansing efficacy of his Son's sacrifice. Such a serious omission is too vital for us to ignore. In the second place, the words which we have placed in italics not only perpetuate the faulty wording of the Westminster Catechism but also convey a misleading conception of the present condition of the Christian. To

speak of 'some remnants of corruption' still remaining i
the believer, necessarily implies that by far the greater pa
of his original corruption has been removed, and that onl
a trifling portion of the same now remains. But somethin
vastly different from *that* is what every true Christia:
discovers to his daily grief and humiliation.

Contrast, dear reader, with the 'some remnants o
corruption' remaining in the Christian (an expressio
frequently found in the writings of the Puritans) the hones
confession of the heavenly-minded Jonathan Edwards:

> 'When I look into my heart and take a view of its wickedness,
> it looks like an abyss infinitely deeper than hell. And it appears
> to me that, were it not for free grace, exalted and raised up
> to the infinite height of all the fullness of the great Jehovah,
> and the arm of his grace stretched forth in all the majesty of
> his power and in all the glory of his sovereignty, I should
> appear sunk down in my sins below hell itself. It is affecting
> to think how ignorant I was when a young Christian, of the
> bottomless depths of wickedness, pride, hypocrisy, and filth
> left in my heart.'

The closer we walk with God, the more conscious will w
be of our utter depravity.

Among the Thirty-nine Articles of the Church of Englanc
(Episcopalian) there is none treating of the importan
doctrine of sanctification! We believe that all the Reformatior
'standards' (creed, confessions and catechisms) will be
searched in vain for any clear statement upon the perfec
holiness which the Church has in Christ or of God's making
him to be, imputatively, sanctification unto his people. In
consequence of this, most theological systems have taugh
that while justification is accomplished the moment the
sinner truly believes in Christ, yet is his sanctification only
then begun, and is a protracted process to be carried or
throughout the remainder of this life by means of the Word
and ordinances, seconded by the discipline of trial and

ffliction. But if this be the case, then there must be a time
n the history of every believer when he is 'justified from all
hings' and yet *unfit* to appear in the presence of God; and
efore he *can* appear there, the process must be completed
he must attain what is called 'entire sanctification' and be
ble to say 'I have no sin', which, according to 1 John 1:8,
vould be the proof of self-deception.

Here, then, is a real dilemma. If we say we have no sin,
ve deceive ourselves; and yet, according to the doctrine of
'progressive sanctification', until we *can* say it (though it
e inarticulately in the moment of death) we are not meet
or the inheritance of the saints in light. What an awful
hought it is, that Christ may come at any hour to those
vho realize that the process of sanctification within them
s *incomplete*. But more: not only are those who have no
complete sanctification unfit for eternal glory, but it would
e daring presumption for them to boldly enter the Holiest
now – the 'new and living way' is not yet available for them,
hey cannot draw near 'with a true heart in full assurance
of faith'. What wonder, then, that those who believe this
doctrine are plunged into perplexity, that such a cloud
rests over their acceptance with God. But thank God, many
triumph over their creed: their hearts are better than their
heads, otherwise their communion with God and their
approach to the throne of his grace would be impossible.

Now in blessed contrast from this inadequate doctrine of
theology, the glorious gospel of God reveals to us a *perfect*
Saviour. It exhibits One who has not only made complete
satisfaction to the righteous Ruler and Judge, providing for
his people a perfect righteousness before him, but whose
sacrifice has also fitted us to worship and serve a holy God
acceptably, and to approach the Father with full confidence
and filial love. A knowledge of the truth of justification is not
sufficient to thus assure the heart: there must be something
more than a realization that the curse of the law is removed

– if the conscience be still defiled, if the eye of God rest upon us as unpurged and unclean, then confidence before him is impossible, for we feel utterly unfit for his ineffable presence. But forever blessed be his name, the precious gospel of God announces that the blood of Christ meet *this* exigency also.

'Now where remission of these (sins) is, there is no more offering for sin. Having therefore, brethren, boldness to enter into the Holiest by the blood of Jesus' (Heb. 10:18, 19). The same sacrifice which has procured the remission of our sins provides the right for us to draw nigh unto God as acceptable worshippers. 'By his own blood he entered in once into the Holy Place, having obtained eternal redemption for us' (Heb. 9:12). Now that which gives the One who took our place *the right* to enter heaven itself, also gives *us* the right to take the *same* place. That which entitled Christ to enter heaven was 'his own blood', and that which entitles the feeblest believer to approach the very throne of God 'with boldness', is 'the blood of Jesus'. Our title to enter heaven *now*, in spirit, is precisely the same *as Christ's* was!

The same precious blood which appeased the wrath of God, covers every stain of sin's guilt and defilement; and not only so, but in the very place of that which it covers and cleanses, it leaves its own excellency; so that because of its infinite purity and merit, the Christian is regarded not only as guiltless and unreprovable, but also as *spotless and holy*. Oh to realize by faith that we are assured of the same welcome by God *now* as his beloved Son received when he sat down at the right hand of the Majesty on high. God views us *in Christ* his 'Holy One', as possessing a holiness as perfect as is the righteousness in which we are accepted, both of them being as perfect as Christ himself. 'In us, as we present ourselves before him through Christ, God *sees no sin*! He looks on us in the face of his Anointed, and there he sees us purer than the heavens' (Alex. Carson).

ts Procurer (Completed)

There is a perfect sanctification in Christ which became ours he moment we first believed in him – little though we *realized* t at the time. There will also be a perfect *conformity* to this *in us*, an actual making good thereof, when we shall be glorified and enter that blessed realm where sin is unknown. In between hese two things is the believer's present life on earth, which consists of a painful and bewildering commingling of lights and shadows, joys and shadows, victories and defeats – the atter *seeming* to greatly preponderate in the cases of many, especially so the longer they live. There is an unceasing warfare between the flesh and the spirit, each bringing forth 'after its own kind', so that groans ever mingle with the Christian's songs. The believer finds himself alternating between thanking God for deliverance from temptation and contritely confessing his deplorable yielding to temptation. Often is he made to cry, 'O wretched man that I am!' (Rom. 7:24). Such has been for upwards of twenty-five years the experience of the writer, as it is still so.

Now just as in the commercial world there are a multitude of medical charlatans announcing sure remedies for the most incurable diseases, and filling their pockets at the expense of those who are foolish enough to believe their fairy-tales; so there are numerous 'quacks' in the religious world, claiming to have a cure for indwelling sin. Such a paragraph as we have just written above would be eagerly seized by these mountebanks, who, casting up hands and eyes of holy horror, would loudly express their pity for such 'a needless tragedy'. They would at once affirm that such an experience, so largely filled with defeat, was because the poor man has never been 'sanctified', and would insist that what he needed to do was 'to lay his all on the altar' and 'receive the second blessing', the 'baptism of the Spirit' or as some call it, 'enter into the victorious life' by fully trusting Christ for victory.'

There are some perverters of the gospel who, in effect represent Christ as only *aiding* sinners to work out a righteousness of their own: they bring in Christ as a mere make-weight to supply their deficiency, or they throw the mantle of his mercy over their failures. Some of the religious quacks we have referred to above would be loud in their outcry against such a travesty of the grace of God in Christ, insisting that we can be justified by nought but his blood. And yet *they* have nothing better to set before their dupes when it comes to 'perfect sanctification' or 'full salvation through fully trusting Jesus'. Christ they say will *aid* us in accomplishing what we have vainly attempted in our own strength, and by fully trusting him we now shall find easy what before we found so arduous. But *God's* Word supplies no warrant to expect sinless perfection in this life, and such teaching can only tend to fatal deception or bitter disappointment.

Those we have referred to above generally separate justification and sanctification both in fact and in time. Yea, they hold that a man may pass through the former and yet be devoid of the latter, and represent them as being attained by two distinct acts of the soul, divided it may be by an interval of years. They exhort Christians to seek sanctification very much as they exhort sinners to seek justification. Those who attain to this 'sanctification', they speak of as being inducted into a superior grade of Christians, having now entered upon 'the *higher* life'. Some refer to this experience as 'the second blessing': by the first, forgiveness of sins is received through faith in the atonement; by the second, we receive deliverance from the power (some add 'the presence') of sin by trusting in the efficacy of Christ's name – a dying Saviour rescues from hell, an ever-living Saviour now delivers from Satan.

The question may be asked, But ought not the Christian to 'present his body a living sacrifice unto God?' Most assuredly, yet *not* for the purpose of *obtaining* sanctification, nor yet for the improving or purifying of 'the flesh', the sinful nature, the 'old man'. The exhortation of Romans 12:1 'as its 'therefore' plainly shows – the 'mercies of God' pointing back to 5:1, 2; 6:5, 6; 8:30, etc.) is a call for us to live in the power of what *is* ours in Christ. The presenting of our bodies 'a living sacrifice to God' is the practical recognition that we *have been* sanctified or consecrated to him, and we are to do so *not* in order to get our bodies sanctified, but in the gracious assurance that they are already 'holy'.

The Christian cannot obtain a right view of the truth of sanctification so long as he separates that blessing from justification, or while he confines his thoughts to a progressive work of grace being wrought within him by the Holy Spirit. 'But ye are washed, but ye *are* sanctified, but ye are justified in the name of the Lord Jesus, and by the Spirit of our God' (1 Cor. 6:11); observe that we are 'sanctified' just as we are 'justified' – in the Name of Another! 'That they may receive forgiveness of sins, and inheritance among them which are sanctified by faith' (Acts 26:18): when we receive the 'forgiveness' of our sins, we also receive 'an inheritance among them that *are* sanctified by faith'. The prayer of Christ, 'Sanctify them through thy truth: thy Word is truth' (John 17:17), is fulfilled as we obtain a spiritual *knowledge* of the truth by the power of the Holy Spirit. It is not by self-efforts, by any 'consecration' of our own, by attempts to 'lay our all on the altar' that we enter into what Christ has procured for his people, but *by faith's appropriation* of what God's Word sets before us.

In Christ, and in him alone, does the believer possess a perfect purity. Christ *has* consecrated us to God by the offering of himself unto him for us. His sacrifice has delivered us from defilement and the ensuing estrangement, and restored us to the favour and fellowship of God. The Father himself views the Christian as identified with and united to his 'Holy One'. There are no degrees and can be no 'progress' in *this* sanctification: an unconverted person is absolutely unholy, and a converted person is absolutely holy. God's standard of holiness is not what the Christian becomes by virtue of the Spirit's work in us here, but what Christ is as seated at his own right hand. Every passage in the New Testament which addresses believers as 'saints' – holy ones – refutes the idea that the believer is not yet sanctified and will not be so until the moment of death.

Nor does the idea of a progressive sanctification, by which the Christian 'more and more dies unto sin', agree with the recorded experience of the most mature saints. The godly John Newton (author of 'How sweet the name of Jesus sounds', etc.) when speaking of the expectations which he cherished at the outset of his Christian life, wrote:

> 'But alas! these my golden expectations have been like South Sea dreams. I have lived hitherto a poor sinner, and I believe I shall die one. Have I, then, gained nothing? Yes, I have gained that which I once would rather have been without – such accumulated proof of the deceitfulness and desperate wickedness of my heart as I hope by the Lord's blessing has, in some measure, taught me to know what I mean when I say, "Behold I am vile!" I was ashamed of myself when I began to serve him, I am more ashamed of myself now, and I expect to be most ashamed of myself when he comes to receive me to himself. But oh! I rejoice in him, that he is not ashamed of me!'

Ah, as the Christian grows in grace, he grows more and more *out of love with himself.*

> 'And thou shalt make a plate of pure gold, and grave upon it, like the engravings of a signet, HOLINESS TO THE LORD. And thou shalt put it on a blue lace, that it may be upon the mitre; upon the forefront of the mitre it shall be. And it shall be upon Aaron's forehead, that Aaron may bear the iniquity of the holy things, which the children of Israel shall hallow in all their holy gifts; and it shall be always upon *his* forehead, that *they* may be accepted of before the LORD' (Exod. 28:36-38).

These verses set before us one of the most precious typical pictures to be found in the Old Testament. Aaron, the high priest, was dedicated and devoted exclusively to the Lord. He served in that office on the behalf of others, as their mediator. He stood before God as the representative of Israel, bearing their names on his shoulders and on his heart (Exod. 28:12, 29). Israel, the people of God, were both represented by and *accepted in* Aaron.

That which was set forth in Exodus 28:36-38 was not a type of 'the way of salvation' but had to do entirely with the approach unto the thrice holy God of his own sinning and failing people. Though the sacrifices offered on the annual day of atonement delivered them from the curse of the law, godly individuals in the nation must have been painfully conscious that *sin* marred their very obedience and defiled their prayers and praises. But through the high priest their service and worship was acceptable to God. The inscription worn on his forehead – 'Holiness to the Lord' – was a solemn appointment by which Israel was impressively taught that holiness became the House of God, and that none who are unholy can possibly draw near unto him. In Leviticus 8:9 the golden plate bearing the inscription is designated 'the holy crown', for it was set over and above all the vestments of Aaron.

Now Aaron foreshadowed Christ as the great High Priest who is 'over the House of God' (Heb. 10:21). Believers are both represented by and accepted in him. The 'Holiness to the Lord' which was '*always*' upon Aaron's head, pointed to the essential holiness of Christ, who '*ever*' liveth to make intercession for us'. Because of our legal and vital union with Christ, *his* holiness is *ours*: the perfections of the great High Priest are the measure of our acceptance with God. Christ has also 'borne the iniquity of our holy things' – made satisfaction for the defects of our worship – so that they are not laid to our charge; the sweet incense of his merits (Rev. 8:3) rendering our worship acceptable to God. By him not only were our sins put away and our persons made acceptable, but our service and worship are rendered pleasing too: 'To offer up spiritual sacrifices, acceptable to God *by Jesus Christ*' (1 Pet. 2:5).

Here, then, is the answer to the pressing question, How can a moral leper be fitted for the presence of God? We need a perfect holiness as well as a perfect righteousness, in order to have access to him. The Holy One cannot look upon sin, and were we to approach him in a way wherein he could not look upon us as being perfectly holy, we could not draw nigh unto him at all. *Christ* is the all-sufficient answer to our every problem, the One who meets our every need. The precious blood of Jesus has separated the believer from all evil, removed all defilement, and made him nigh unto God in all the acceptableness of his Son. How vastly different is this from that conception which limits sanctification to our experiences and attainments! How definitely better is God's way to man's way, and how far are his thoughts on this above ours!

Now it is in the New Testament epistles that we are shown most fully the reality and substance of what was typed out under Judaism. First, we read, 'For both he that sanctifieth and they who are sanctified are all of one' (Heb. 2:11). Christ is both our sanctification and our sanctifier. He is our sanctifier, first, by his blood putting away our sins and cleansing us from all defilement. Second, by the operations of the Holy Spirit, for whatever he doth, he does *as* 'the Spirit of Christ' who procured him (Ps. 68:18 and Acts 2:33) for his people. Third, by communicating a holy life unto us (John 10:10): the whole stock of grace and holiness is in his hands, he communicating the same unto his people (John 1:16). Fourth, by appearing in heaven as our representative: *he* being 'Holiness to the Lord' *for us*. Fifth, by applying and blessing his Word to his people, so that they are washed thereby (Eph. 5:26). He is our sanctification because the holiness of his nature, as well as his obedience, is imputed to us (1 Cor. 1:30)

'We are sanctified through the offering of the body of Jesus Christ once for all' (Heb. 10:10). The Christian will never have right thoughts on this subject until he perceives that his sanctification *before God* was accomplished at Calvary. As we read, 'And you, that were sometime alienated and enemies in your mind by wicked works, yet now hath he reconciled in the body of his flesh through death, to present you *holy* and unblameable and unreprovable in his sight' (Col. 1:21, 22): By his work at the cross, Christ presents the Church unto God in all the excellency of his perfect sacrifice. In these passages it is not at all a question of any work which is wrought *in* us, but of what Christ's oblation has secured *for us*. By virtue of his sacrifice, believers have been set apart unto God in all Christ's purity and merits, a sure title being accorded them for heaven. God accounts us holy according to the holiness of Christ's sacrifice, the full value of which rests upon the least instructed, the feeblest, and most tried Christian on earth.

So infinitely sufficient is Christ's oblation for us that 'by one offering he hath perfected forever them that are sanctified' (Heb. 10:14). As we read again, 'Ye are *complete* in Him' (Col. 2:10), and this, because his work was complete. *All* true believers are in the everlasting purpose of God, and in the actual accomplishment of that purpose by the Lord Jesus, perfectly justified and perfectly sanctified. But all believers are not *aware* of that blessed fact; far from it. Many are confused and bewildered on this subject. One reason for that is, that so many are looking almost entirely to human teachers for instructions, instead of relying upon the Holy Spirit to guide them into the truth, and searching the Scriptures for a knowledge of the same. The religious world today is a veritable 'Babel of tongues', and all certainty is at an end if we turn away from the Word (failing to make *it* our *chief* study) and lean upon preachers. Alas, how many in professing Protestantism are little better off than the poor Papists, who receive unquestioningly what the 'priest' tells them.

It is only as we read God's Word, mixing faith therewith (Heb. 4:2) and appropriating the same unto ourselves, that the Christian can enter into *God's* thoughts concerning him. In the sacred Scriptures, and nowhere else, can the believer discover what God has made Christ to be unto him and what he has made him to be in Christ. So too it is in the Scriptures, and nowhere else, that we can learn the truth about *ourselves*, that 'in the flesh (what we are by nature as the depraved descendants of fallen Adam) there dwelleth *no* good thing' (Rom. 7:18). Until we learn to distinguish (as God does) between the 'I' and the 'sin which dwelleth in me' (Rom. 7:20) there can be no settled peace. Scripture knows nothing of the sanctification of 'the old man', and as long as we are hoping for any improvement in him we are certain to meet with disappointment. If we are to 'worship God in the Spirit' and '*rejoice* in Christ Jesus' we must learn to have '*no* confidence in the flesh' (Phil. 3:3).

'Wherefore Jesus, also, that he might sanctify the people with his own blood, suffered without the gate' (Heb. 13:12). The precious blood of Christ has done more than simply make expiation for their sins: it has also set them apart to God as his people. It is that which has brought them *into fellowship* with the Father himself. By the shedding of his blood for us, Christ made it consistent with the honour and holiness of God to take us as his peculiar people; it also procured the Holy Spirit who has (by regeneration) fitted us for the privileges and duties of our high calling. Thus, Christ has sanctified his people both objectively and subjectively. We are 'sanctified with his own blood', first, as it was an *oblation* to God; second, as its *merits* are imputed to us; third, as its *efficacy* is applied to us.

Christ's blood 'cleanseth us from all sin' (1 John 1:7) in a threefold way. First, Godwards, by blotting out our sins and removing our defilement from his view (as judge). Second, by procuring the Holy Spirit, by whom we receive 'the *washing* of regeneration' (Titus 3:5). Third, by our consciences being 'purged' (Heb. 9:14) as *faith lays hold of* these blessed facts, and thus we are fitted to 'serve the living God!' Herein we may perceive how God puts the fullest honour on his beloved Son, by making him not only the repairer of our ruin and the triumphant undoer of the serpent's work (1 John 3:8), but also giving us his own perfect standing before God and communicating his own holy nature unto his people – for a branch cannot be in the true vine without partaking of its life.

In the person of Christ God beholds a holiness which abides his closest scrutiny, yea, which rejoices and satisfies his heart; and whatever Christ is before God, he is for his people – 'whither the Forerunner is *for us* entered' (Heb. 6:20), '*now* to appear in the presence of God *for us*' (Heb. 9:24)! In Christ's holiness we are meet for that place unto which divine grace has exalted us, so that we are 'made to sit together in the heavenlies in Christ Jesus' (Eph. 2:6). This is not accomplished by any experience, separated by a long process from our justification, but is a blessed fact since the moment we first believed on Christ. We are in Christ, and how can any one be *in him*, and yet not be perfectly sanctified? From the first moment we were 'joined to the Lord' (1 Cor. 6:17), we are '*holy* brethren, partakers of the heavenly calling' (Heb. 3:1). *This* is what the Christian's faith needs to lay hold of and rest on, upon the authority of him that cannot lie. Nevertheless, the best taught, the most spiritual and mature Christian, apprehends the truth but feebly and inadequately, for now 'we see through a glass darkly'.

True, there *is* such a thing as a growth *in the knowledge of* our sanctification, that is, providing our thoughts are

137

formed by the Word of God. There is an experimental entering into the practical enjoyment of what God has made Christ to be unto us, so that by faith therein our thoughts and habits, affections and associations are affected thereby. There is such a thing as our apprehending the glorious standing and state which divine grace has given us in the Beloved, and exhibiting the influence of the same upon our character and conduct. But *that* is not what we are *here* treating of. That which we are now considering is the wondrous and glorious fact that the Christian was as completely sanctified in God's view the first moment he laid hold of Christ by faith, as he will be when every vestige of sin has disappeared from his person, and he stands before him glorified in spirit and soul and body.

But the question may be asked, What provision has God made to meet the needs of his people sinning *after* they are sanctified? This falls not within the compass of the present aspect of our subject. Yet briefly, the answer is, The ministry of Christ on high as our great High Priest (Heb. 7:26) and Advocate (1 John 2:1); and their penitently confessing their sins, which secures their forgiveness and cleansing (1 John 1:9). The sins of the Christian mar his communion with God and hinder his enjoyment of his salvation, but they affect not his standing and state in Christ. If I judge not myself for my sinful failures and falls, the chastening rod will descend upon me, yet wielded not by an angry God, but by my loving Father (Heb. 12:5-11).

We are not unmindful of the fact that there is not a little in this chapter which worldly-minded professors may easily pervert to their own ruin – what truth of Scripture is not capable of being 'wrested'? But that is no reason why God's people should be *deprived* of one of the choicest and most nourishing portions of the Bread of Life! Other chapters in this book are thoroughly calculated to 'preserve the balance of truth'.

9

Its Securer

The Christian has been sanctified by the triune Jehovah:
infinite wisdom and fathomless grace so ordered it that
he is indebted to each of the Eternal Three. The Lord God
designed that all the Persons in the blessed Trinity should
be honoured in the making holy of his people, so that each
of Them might be distinctively praised by us. First, the
Father sanctified his people by an eternal decree, choosing
them in Christ before the foundation of the world and
predestinating them unto the adoption of children. Second,
the Son sanctified his people by procuring for them a perfect
and inalienable standing before the Judge of all, the infinite
merits of his finished work being reckoned to their account.
Third, God the Spirit makes good the Father's decree and
imparts to them what the work of Christ procured for them:
the Spirit is the actual Securer of sanctification, *applying it*
to their persons. Thus the believer has abundant cause to
adore and glorify the Father, the Son, and the Holy Spirit.

It is very remarkable to observe the perfect harmony
there is between the different operations of the Eternal
Three in connection with the making holy of the elect, and
the threefold signification of the term 'sanctification'. In
an earlier chapter we furnished proof that the word 'to
sanctify' has a three-fold meaning, namely, to separate,

to cleanse, to adorn. First in Scripture a person or thing is said to be sanctified when it is consecrated or set apart from a common to a sacred use. So in the eternal decree of the Father, the elect were separated in the divine mind from countless millions of our race which were to be created and set apart for his own delight and glory. Second, where those persons and things are unclean, they must be purified so as to *fit* them for God's pleasure and use. That was the specific work assigned to the Son: his precious blood has provided the means for our purification. Third, the persons or things sanctified need to be beautiful and adorned for God's service: this is accomplished by the Holy Spirit.

It is also striking and blessed to note the relation and order of the several acts of the Holy Three in connection with our sanctification. The *source* of it is 'the eternal purpose' or decree of God: 'by the which *will* we are sanctified' (Heb. 10:10). The *substance* of it was brought forth by Christ when he fully accomplished God's will on our behalf: 'that he might sanctify the people with his own blood' (Heb. 13:12). The *securer* of it is the Holy Spirit, who by his works of grace within applies to the individual the sanctification which the Church has in its Head: 'being sanctified by the Holy Spirit' (Rom. 15:16). It is not until the Comforter takes up his abode in the heart that the Father's will begins to be actualized and the Son's 'work' evidences its efficacy toward us. This glorious gift, then, is let down to us from the Father, through the Son, by the Spirit.

If we consider the nature of Christ's work for his people and the perfection of their standing in him before God, it could not for a moment be supposed that this having been accomplished by the grace, wisdom, and power of God, that their *state* should be left unaffected – that their position should be so gloriously changed, yet their condition remain as sinful as ever; that they should be left in their sins to take comfort from their immunity to divine wrath. The degradation, pollution, and utter ruin of our nature; our estrangement from God, spiritual death, and our whole heritage of woe are the immediate consequences of *sin*. And what would forgiveness, justification, and redemption in Christ mean, if *deliverance from* all those consequences did not directly and necessarily follow? Our being made the righteousness of God in Christ (2 Cor. 5:21) would be but an empty name, if it does not imply and entail recovery from all that sin had forfeited and deliverance from all that sin had incurred. Thank God *that*, in the end (when we are glorified), will be perfectly effected.

It is true that when Christ first seeks out his people he finds them entirely destitute of holiness, yea, of even desire after it; but he does not leave them in that awful state. No, such would neither honour him nor fulfil the Father's will. Glorious as is the triumph of divine grace in the justification of a sinner, through the work of Christ as Surety, yet even that must be regarded as a means to an end. See how this is brought out in every scriptural statement of the purpose of grace concerning the redeemed, or the design of the mission and suffering of the Redeemer: 'I am come that they might have life, and that they might have it more abundantly' (John 10:10); 'Who gave himself for us, that he might redeem us from all iniquity, and purify unto himself a peculiar people, zealous of good works' (Titus 2:14); 'Whereby are given unto us exceeding great and precious promises: that by these ye might be partakers of the divine nature, having escaped the corruption that is in the world through lust' (2 Pet. 1:4); 'Behold what manner of love the Father hath bestowed upon us, that we should be called the sons of God' (1 John 3:1).

Since we are made the righteousness of God in Christ the result of this in the Christian, must, ultimately, correspond with that perfection. In other words, nothing short of perfect fellowship with the Father and with his Son can answer to his

141

having died on account of our sins and risen again on account of our justification; and having risen, become the Head and Source of an entirely new life to all who believe on him. The aim of the Father's love and of the Son's grace, was not only that we might have restored to us the life which we lost in Adam, but that we should have 'life more abundantly'; that we should be brought back not merely to the position of servants – which was the status of unfallen Adam – but be given the wondrous place of sons; that we should be fitted not simply for an earthly paradise, but for an eternity of joy in the immediate presence of God in heaven.

Now it is on the ground of what Christ did and earned for his people, and with a view to the realization of the Father's purpose of their glorification, that the Holy Spirit is given to the elect. And it makes much for his praise and for their peace that they obtain a clear and comprehensive view of his work within them; nor can that be secured by a hurried or superficial study of the subject. His operations are varied and manifold; yet all proceeding from one foundation and all advancing toward one grand end. That which we are now to consider is the 'sanctification of the Spirit', an expression which is found both in 2 Thessalonians 2:13 and 1 Peter 1:2. The connection in which the expression occurs in the two passages just mentioned, clearly intimates that the sanctification of the Spirit is an integral part of our salvation, that it is closely associated with our 'belief of the truth', and that it precedes our practical obedience.

John Owen's definition of the Spirit's sanctification, based on 1 Thessalonians 5:23 is as follows:

'Sanctification is an immediate work of the Spirit of God on the souls of believers, purifying and cleansing of their natures from the pollution and uncleanness of sin, renewing in them the image of God, and thereby enabling them from a spiritual and habitual principle of grace, to yield obedience unto God, according unto the tenor and terms of the new covenant, by virtue of the life and death of Jesus Christ. Or more briefly: it is the universal renovation of our natures by the Holy Spirit, into the image of God, through Jesus Christ.'

Full and clear though this definition be, we humbly conceive it is both inadequate and inaccurate: inadequate, because it leaves out several essential elements; inaccurate, because it confounds the effects with the cause. Later, he says:

'In the sanctification of believers the Holy Spirit doth work in them, in their whole souls – their minds, wills, and affections – a gracious, supernatural habit, principle, and disposition of living unto God, wherein the substance or essence, the life and being, of holiness doth consist.'

In an article thereon S. E. Pierce said:

'Sanctification, or gospel-holiness, without which no man shall see the Lord, comprehends the whole work of the Spirit of God within and upon us, from our regeneration to our eternal glorification. It is the fruit and blessed consequence of his indwelling us, and the continued effect of spiritual regeneration, i.e., in begetting within us a nature suited to take in spiritual things, and be properly affected by them. Regeneration is the root and sanctification is the bud, blossom and fruit which it produces. In our regeneration by the Holy Spirit we are made alive to God, and this is manifested by our faith in Christ Jesus. Our lusts are mortified because we are quickened together with Christ. And what we style the sanctification of the Spirit, which follows after regeneration hath taken place within us, consists in drawing forth that spiritual life which is conveyed to our souls in our new birth, into acts and exercise on Christ and spiritual things, in quickening our graces, and in leading us to walk in the paths of holiness, by which proof is given that we are alive to God through Jesus Christ our Lord.'

This, we believe is preferable to Owens, yet still leaving something to be desired.

Exactly what is the sanctification of the Spirit? Personally, we very much doubt whether that question can be satisfactorily answered in a single sentence, for in framing one, account needs to be taken of the change which is produced in the believing sinner's relationship to God, his relationship to God, his relationship to the unregenerate, and his relationship to the divine law. *Positionally*, our sanctification by the Spirit results from our being vitally united to Christ, for the moment we are livingly joined to him, his holiness becomes ours, and our standing before God is the same as his. *Relatively*, our sanctification of the Spirit issues from our being renewed by him, for the moment he quickens us we are set apart from those who are dead in sins. Personally, we are consecrated unto God by the Spirit's indwelling us, making our bodies his temples. *Experimentally*, our sanctification of the Spirit consists in the impartation to us of a principle ('nature') of holiness, whereby we become conformed to the divine law. Let us consider each of these viewpoints separately.

Our union to Christ is the grand hinge on which everything turns. Divorced from him, we have nothing spiritually. Describing our unregenerate condition, the apostle says, 'at that time ye were without Christ', and being without him, it necessarily follows 'being aliens from the commonwealth of Israel, and strangers from the covenants of promise, having no hope, and without God in the world' (Eph. 2:12). But the moment the Holy Spirit makes us livingly one with Christ, all that he has becomes ours, we are then 'joint-heirs with Him'. Just as a woman obtains the right to share all that a man has once she is wedded to him, so a poor sinner becomes holy before God the moment he is vitally united to the Holy One. Everything which God requires from us, everything which is needed by us, is treasured up for us in Christ.

By our union with Christ we receive a new and holy nature, whereby we are capacitated for holy living, which holy living is determined and regulated by our practical and experimental fellowship with him. By virtue of our federal union with the first Adam we not only had imputed to us the guilt of his disobedience, but we also received from him the sinful nature which has vitiated our souls, powerfully influencing all our faculties. In like manner, by virtue of our federal union with the last Adam, the elect not only have imputed to them the righteousness of his obedience, but they also receive from him (by the Spirit) a holy nature, which renews all the faculties of their souls and powerfully affects their actions. Once we become united to the Vine, the life and holy virtue which is in him flows into us, and brings forth spiritual fruit. Thus, the moment the Spirit unites us to Christ, we are 'sanctified in Christ Jesus' (1 Cor. 1:2).

It is axiomatic that those whom God separates unto himself must be suited to himself, that is, they must be holy. Equally clear is it from the Scriptures that, whatsoever God does he is determined that the crown of honour for it should rest upon the head of Christ, for he is the grand Centre of all the divine counsels. Now both of these fundamental considerations are secured by God's making us partakers of his own holiness, through creating us anew in Christ Jesus. God will neither receive nor own any one who has the least taint of sin's defilement upon him, and it is only as we are made new creatures in Christ that we can fully measure up to the unalterable requirements of God. Our *state* must be holy as well as our *standing*; and as we showed in the last three chapters Christ himself is our sanctification, so now we seek to point out that we are actually sanctified *in Christ* – personally and vitally.

'But of him are ye in Christ Jesus' (1 Cor. 1:30) – 'of Him' by the power and quickening operation of the Spirit. Christians are supernaturally and livingly incorporated with Christ. 'For we are his workmanship, *created in* Christ Jesus' (Eph. 2:10): that new creation is accomplished in our union with his person. This is our spiritual *state*: a 'new man' has

145

been 'created in righteousness and true holiness' (Eph. 4:24), and this we are exhorted to 'put on' or make manifest. This is not at all a matter of progress or attainment, but is true of every Christian the moment he is born again. The terms 'created in righteousness (our justification) and true holiness' (our sanctification) describe what the 'new man' is in Christ. It is not simply something which we are to pursue – though that is true, and is intimated in the 'put ye on'; but it is what all Christians actually are: their sanctification in Christ is an accomplished fact: it is just because Christians are 'saints' they are to lead saintly lives.

The believer *begins* his Christian life by having been perfectly sanctified in Christ. Just as both our standing and state were radically affected by virtue of our union with the first Adam, so *both* our standing and state are completely changed by virtue of our union with the last Adam. As the believer has a perfect standing in holiness before God because of his federal union with Christ, so his state is perfect before God, because he is now vitally united to Christ: he is in Christ, and Christ is in him. By the regenerating operation of the Spirit we are 'joined unto the Lord' (1 Cor. 6:17). The moment they were born again, *all* Christians were sanctified in Christ with a sanctification to which no growth in grace, no attainments in holy living, can add one iota. Their sanctification, like their justification, is 'complete in him' (Col. 2:10). Christ himself is their life, and he becomes such by a personal union to himself which nothing can dissolve. From the moment of his new birth every child of God is a 'saint in Christ Jesus' (Rom. 1:7), one of the 'holy brethren' (Heb. 3:1); and it is just because they are such, they are called upon to live holy lives. O what cause we have to adore the grace, the wisdom, and the power of God!

When one of God's elect is quickened into newness of life a great change is made *relatively*, that is, in connection with his relation to his fellowmen. Previously, he too was both in the world and of it, being numbered with the ungodly, and enjoying their fellowship. But at regeneration he is born unto a new family, even the living family of God, and henceforth his standing is no longer among those who are 'without Christ': 'Who hath delivered us from the power of darkness, and hath translated us into the kingdom of his dear Son' (Col. 1:13). Thus, when one is made alive in Christ by the Holy Spirit, he at once becomes *separated* from those who are dead in trespasses and sins and therefore this is another aspect of the 'sanctification of the Spirit'. This was typed out of old. When the Lord was revealed unto Abraham, the word to him was '*Get thee out* of thy country, and from thy kindred' (Gen. 12:1). So again it was with Israel: no sooner were they delivered from the angel of death by the blood of the lamb, than they were required to leave Egypt behind them.

Personally we are sanctified or consecrated unto God by the Spirit's indwelling us and making our bodies his temples. As he came upon Christ himself ('without measure') so, in due time, he is given to each of his members: 'ye have an unction (the Spirit) from the Holy One' – Christ; 'the anointing (the Spirit) which ye have received of him (Christ) abideth in you' (1 John 2:20, 27) – it is from this very fact we receive our name, for 'Christian' means 'an *anointed* one', the term being taken from the type in Psalm 133:2. It is the indwelling presence of the Holy Spirit which constitutes a believer a holy person. That which made Canaan the 'holy' land, Jerusalem the 'holy' city, the temple the 'holy' place, was the *presence* and appearing of the Holy One there! And that which makes any man 'holy' is the perpetual abiding of the Spirit within him. Needless to say, his indwelling of us necessarily produces fruits of holiness in heart and life – this will come before us in the sequel.

147

Amazing, blessed, the glorious fact, the Holy Spirit indwells the regenerate so that their bodies become the temples of the living God.

> 'The Holy Spirit descends on them and enters within them, *in consequence of* their union with Christ. He comes from heaven to make known this union between Christ and them. He is the divine *manifester* of it. He dwells in us as a well of water springing up into everlasting life. He abides with us as our divine Comforter, and will be our guide even unto death, and continue his life-giving influences in us and dwell in us, filling us with all the fullness of God in heaven for ever' (S. E. Pierce).

This indwelling of the Spirit is, in the order of God, subsequent to and in consequence of our being sanctified by the blood of Jesus; for it is obvious that God could not 'dwell' in those who were standing under the imputation of their guilt. The Holy Spirit, therefore, from the very fact of making our bodies his temples, attests and evidences the completeness and perpetuity of the sanctification which is ours by the sacrifice of Christ. He comes to us not to procure blessings which Christ hath already purchased for us, but to make them known to us: 'Now we have received, not the spirit of the world, but the Spirit which is of God; that we might know the things that are freely given to us of God' (1 Cor. 2:12). He comes to sustain those in whom the life of Christ now is.

Its Securer (Completed)

'Sanctification of the Spirit' (2 Thess. 2:13) is a comprehensive expression which has a fourfold significance at least. First, it points to that supernatural operation of the Spirit whereby a sinner is 'created in Christ Jesus' (Eph. 2:10), made vitally one with him, and thereby a partaker of his holiness. Second, it tells of the vital change which this produces in his relation to the ungodly: having been quickened into newness of life, he is at once separated from those who are dead in sins, so that both as to his standing and state he is no longer with them common to Satan, sin and the world. Third, it speaks of the Spirit himself taking up his abode in the quickened soul, thereby rendering him personally holy. Fourth, it refers to his bringing the heart into conformity with the divine law, with all that that connotes. Before taking up this last point, we will offer a few more remarks upon the third.

The coming of this divine and glorious Person to indwell one who is depraved and sinful is both a marvel and a mystery: a marvel that he should, a mystery that he would. How is it possible for him who is ineffably holy to dwell within those who are so unholy? Not a few have said it is impossible, and were it not for the plain declarations of Scripture thereon, probably all of us would come to the same conclusion. But God's ways are very different from ours, and his love and grace have achieved that which our poor hearts had never conceived of. This has been clearly recognized in connection with the amazing birth, and the still more amazing death of Christ; but it has not been so definitely perceived in connection with the descent of the Spirit to indwell believers.

There is a striking analogy between the advent to this earth of the second person of the Trinity and the advent of the third person, and the marvel and mystery of the one should prepare us for the other. Had the same not become an historical fact, who among us had ever supposed that the Father had suffered his beloved Son to enter such depths of degradation as he did? Who among us had ever imagined that the Lord of glory would lie in a manger? But he did! In view of that; why should we be so staggered at the concept of the Holy Spirit's entering our poor hearts? As the Father was pleased to allow the glory of the Son to be eclipsed for a season by the degradation into which he descended, so in a very real sense he suffers the glory of the Spirit to be hid for a season by the humiliation of his tabernacling in our bodies.

It is on the ground of Christ's work that the Spirit comes to us.

'Whatever we receive here is but the result of the fullness given to us in Christ. If the Spirit comes to dwell in us as the Spirit of peace, it is because Jesus by his blood, once offered, hath secured for us that peace. If the Spirit comes as the Spirit of glory, it is because Jesus has entered into and secured glory for us. If the Spirit comes as the Spirit of sonship, it is because Jesus has returned for us to the bosom of the Father and brought us into the nearness of the same love. If the Spirit comes to us as the Spirit of life, it is because of the life hidden for us in Christ with God. The indwelling of the Spirit therefore being a result of the abiding relation to God into which the resurrection and ascension of our Lord has brought us, must of necessity be an abiding presence. Consequently, the sanctification which results from the fact of his presence in us and from the fact of the new man being created in us, must be a complete and abiding sanctification – as complete and as abiding as the relation which Christ holds to us in redemption as the Representative and Head of his mystical body' (B. W. Newton).

Yet let it be pointed out that the blessed Spirit does not allow our hearts to remain in the awful condition in which he first finds them; and this brings us to our fourth point. In Titus 3:5 we read 'according to his mercy he saved us, by the washing or regeneration, and renewing of the Holy Spirit'. All that is comprehended in this 'washing' we may not be able to say, but it certainly includes the casting of all idols out of our hearts, to such an extent that God now occupies the throne of our hearts. By this 'washing of regeneration' the soul is so cleansed from its native pollution that sin is no longer delighted in, but hated: and the affections are raised from things below unto things above. We are well aware of the fact that this is the particular point which most exercises honest consciences; yet, God does not intend that our difficulties should be so cleared up in this life that all exercise of heart should be at an end.

Though it be true that the flesh remains unaltered in the Christian, and that at times its activities are such that our evidences of regeneration are clouded over, yet it remains that a great change was wrought in us at the new birth, the effects of which abide. Though it be true that a sea of corruption still dwells within, and that at times sin rages violently, and so prevails that it seems a mockery to conclude that we have been delivered from its domination; yet this does not alter the fact that a miracle of grace has been wrought within us. Though the Christian is conscious of so much filth within, he has experienced the 'washing of regeneration'. Before the new birth he saw no beauty in Christ that he should desire him; but now he views him as 'the Fairest among ten thousand'. Before, he loved those like himself; but now he 'loves the brethren' (1 John 3:14). Moreover, his understanding has been cleansed from many polluting errors and heresies. Finally, it is a fact that the main stream of his desires runs out after God.

But 'the washing of regeneration' is only the negative side: positively there is 'the renewing of the Holy Spirit'. Though this 'renewing' falls far short of what will take place in the saint at his glorification, yet it is a very real and radical experience. A great change and renovation is made in the soul, which has a beneficial effect upon all of its faculties. This 'renewing of the Holy Spirit' has in it a transforming power, so that the heart and mind are brought into an obediential frame toward God. The soul is now able to discern that God's will is the most 'good, and acceptable, and perfect' (Rom. 12:2) of all, and there is a deep desire and a sincere effort made to become conformed thereto. But let it be carefully noted that the present and not the past tense is employed in Titus 3:5 – not ye were washed and renewed, but a 'washing' and 'renewing': it is a continual work of the Spirit.

Ere proceeding to show further the nature of the Spirit's work in the soul in his sanctifying operations, let it be pointed out that what our hearts most need to lay hold of and rest on is that which has been before us in the last few chapters. The believer has already been perfectly sanctified in the decree and purpose of the Father. Christ has wrought out for him that which, when reckoned to his account, perfectly fits him for the courts of God's temple above. The moment he is quickened by the Spirit he is 'created in Christ', and therefore 'sanctified in Christ'; thus both his standing and state are holy in God's sight. Furthermore, the Spirit's indwelling him, making his body his temple, constitutes him personally holy – just as the presence of God in the temple made Canaan the 'holy land' and Jerusalem the 'holy city'.

It is of the very first importance that the Christian should be thoroughly clear upon this point. We do not become saints by holy actions – that is the fundamental error of all false religions. No we must first be saints before there can be any holy actions, as the fountain must be pure before its stream can be, the tree good if its fruit is to be wholesome. The order of Scripture is 'Let it not be once named among you, as becometh saints' (Eph. 5:3), and 'but now are ye light in the Lord: walk as children of light' (Eph. 5:8); 'in behaviour as becometh holiness' (Titus 2:3). God first sets our hearts at rest, before he bids our hands engage in his service. He gives life, that we may be capacitated to render love. He creates in us a sanctified nature, that there may be sanctified conduct. God presents us spotless in the Holiest of all according to the blood of sprinkling, that, coming forth with a conscience purged from dead works, we may seek to please and glorify him.

It is the creating of this holy nature within us that we must next consider.

'It is something that is holy, both in its principle, and in its actions; and is superior to anything that can come from man, or be performed by himself. It does not lie in a conformity to the light of nature, and the dictates of it; nor is it what may go by the name of moral virtue, which was exercised by some of the heathen philosophers, to a very great degree, and yet they had not a grain of holiness in them; but were full of the lusts of envy, pride, revenge, etc., nor does it lie in a bare, external conformity to the law of God, or in an outward reformation of life and manners: this appeared in the Pharisees to a great degree, who were pure in their own eyes, and thought themselves holier than others, and disdained them, and yet their hearts were full of all manner of impurity.

'Nor is it what is called restraining grace: persons may be restrained by the injunction of parents and masters, by the laws of magistrates, and by the ministry of the Word, from the grosser sins of life; and be preserved, by the providence of God, from the pollutions of the world, and yet not be sanctified. Nor are gifts, ordinary or extraordinary, sanctifying grace: Judas Iscariot no doubt had both, the ordinary gifts of a preacher, and the extraordinary gifts of an apostle; yet he was not a holy man. Gifts are not graces: a man may have all gifts and all knowledge, and speak with the tongue of men, and angels, and not have grace; there may be a silver tongue where there is an unsanctified heart. Nor is sanctification a restoration of the lost image of Adam, or an amendment of that image marred by the sin of man; or a new vamping up of the old principles of nature' (John Gill).

Having seen what this holy nature, imparted by the Spirit, is not, let us endeavour to define what it is. It is something entirely new: a new creation, a new heart, a new spirit, a new man, the conforming of us to another image, even to that of the last Adam, the Son of God. It is the impartation of a holy principle, implanted in the midst of corruption, like a lovely rosebush growing out of a dung-heap. It is the carrying forward of that 'good work' begun in us at regeneration (Phil. 1:6). It is called by many names, such as 'the inward man' (2 Cor. 4:16) and 'the hidden man of the heart' (1 Pet. 3:4), not only because it has its residence in the soul, but because our fellows can see it not. It is designated 'seed' (1 John 3:9) and 'spirit' (John 3:6) because it is wrought in us by the Spirit of God. It is likened to a 'root' (Job 19:28), to 'good treasure of the heart' (Matt. 12:35), to 'oil in the vessel' (Matt. 25:4) – by 'oil' there is meant grace, so called for its illuminating nature in giving discernment to the understanding, and for its supplying and softening nature, taking off the hardness from the heart and the stubbornness from the will.

It is in this aspect of our sanctification that we arrive at the third meaning of the term: the blessed Spirit not only separates from the common herd of the unregenerate, cleanses our hearts from the pollution of sin, but he suitably adorns the temple in which he now dwells. This he does by making us partakers of 'the divine nature' (2 Pet. 1:4), which is a positive thing, the communication of a holy principle, whereby we are 'renewed after the image of God'. When the Levites were to minister in the holy place, not only were they required to wash themselves, but to put on their priestly attire and ornaments, which were comely and beautiful. In like manner, believers are a holy and royal priesthood (1 Pet. 2:5), for they have not only been washed from the filth of sin, but are 'all glorious within' (Ps. 45:13). They have not only had the robe of imputed righteousness put upon them (Isa. 61:10), but the beautifying grace of the Spirit has been implanted in them.

It is by the reception of this holy principle or nature that the believer is freed from the domination of sin and brought into the liberty of righteousness, though not until death is he delivered from the plague and presence of sin. At their justification believers obtain a relative or judicial sanctification, which provides for them a perfect standing before God, by which they receive proof of their covenant relationship with him, that they are his peculiar people, his 'treasure', his 'portion'. But more, they are also inherently sanctified in their persons by a gracious work of the Spirit within their souls. They are 'renewed' throughout the whole of their beings; for as the poison of sin was diffused throughout the entire man, so is grace. It helps not a little to perceive that, as Thomas Boston pointed out long ago in his *Human Nature in its Fourfold State*: 'Holiness is not one grace only, but all the graces of the Spirit: it is a constellation of graces; it is all the graces in their seed and root.'

Yet let it be pointed out that, though the whole of the Christian's person is renewed by the Spirit, and all the faculties of his soul are renovated, nevertheless, there is no operation of grace upon his old nature, so that its evil is expelled: the 'flesh' or principle of indwelling sin is neither eradicated nor purified nor made good. Our 'old man' (which must be distinguished from the soul and its faculties) is 'corrupt according to the deceitful lusts', and remains so till the end of our earthly pilgrimage, ever striving against the 'spirit' or principle of holiness or 'new man'. As the soul at the very first moment of its union with the body (in the womb) became sinful, so it is not until the moment of its dissolution from the body that the soul becomes inherently sinless. As an old divine quaintly said, 'Sin brought death into the world, and God, in a way of holy resentment, makes use of death to put an end to the very being of sin in his saints.'

Many readers will realize that we are here engaged in grappling with a difficult and intricate point. No man is competent to give such a clear and comprehensive description of our inward sanctification that all difficulty is cleared up: the most he can do is to point out what it is not, and then seek to indicate the direction in which its real nature is to be sought. As a further effort toward this it may be said that, this principle of holiness which the Spirit imparts to the believer consists of spiritual light, whereby the heart is (partly) delivered from the darkness in which

155

the Fall enveloped it. It is such an opening of the eyes of our understandings that we are enabled to see spiritual things and discern their excellency; for before we are sanctified by the Spirit we are totally blind to their reality and beauty: such passages as John 1:5; Acts 26:18; 2 Corinthians 4:6; Ephesians 5:8; Colossians 1:13; 1 Peter 2:9 (read them!) make this clear.

Further, that principle of holiness which the Spirit imparts to the believer consists of spiritual life. Previous to its reception the soul is in a state of spiritual death, that is, it is alienated from and incapacitated toward God. At our renewing by the Spirit, we receive a vital principle of spiritual life: compare John 5:24; 10:11, 28; Romans 8:2; Ephesians 2:1. It is by this new life we are capacitated for communion with and obedience to God. One more; that principle of holiness consists of spiritual love. The natural man is in a state of enmity with God; but at regeneration there is implanted that which delights in and cleaves to God: compare Deuteronomy 30:6; Romans 5:5; Galatians 5:24. As 'light' this principle of holiness affects the understanding, as 'life' it influences and moves the will, as 'love' it directs and moulds the affections. Thus, also it partakes of the very nature of him who is Light, Life and Love. 'Let the beauty of the LORD be upon us' (Ps. 90:17) signifies 'let this principle of holiness (as light, life and love) be healthy within and made manifest through and by us.

But we must now turn to the most important aspect of all, of the nature of this principle of holiness, whereby the Spirit sanctified us inherently. Our experimental sanctification consists in our hearts being conformed to the divine law. This should be so obvious that no laboured argument should be required to establish the fact. As all sin is a transgression of the law (1 John 3:4), so all holiness must be a fulfilling of the law. The natural man is not subject to the law, neither indeed can he be (Rom. 8:7). Why? Because he is devoid of that principle from which acceptable obedience to the law can proceed. The great requirement of the law is love: love to God, and love to our neighbour; but regarding the unregenerate it is written, 'ye have not the love of God in you' (John 5:42). Hence it is that God's promise to his elect is 'The LORD thy God will circumcise thine heart, and the heart of thy seed, to love the LORD thy God with all thine heart' (Deut. 30:6) – for 'love is the fulfilling of the law'.

This is the grand promise of the Covenant: 'I will put my laws into their mind, and write them in their hearts' (Heb. 8:10); and again, 'I will put my Spirit within you, and cause you to walk in my statutes' (Ezek. 36:27). As we said in the preceding article: when Christ comes to his people he finds them entirely destitute of holiness, and of every desire after it; but he does not leave them in that awful condition. No, he sends forth the Holy Spirit, communicates to them a sincere love for God, and imparts to them a principle of 'nature' which delights in his ways. 'They that are in the flesh cannot please God' (Rom. 8:8). Why? Because any work to be pleasing to him *must* proceed from a right principle (love to him), be performed by a right rule (his law, or revealed will), and have a right end in view (his glory); and this is only made possible by the sanctification of the Spirit.

Experimental holiness is conformity of heart and life to the divine law. The law of God is 'holy, just and good' (Rom. 7:12), and therefore does it require inward righteousness or conformity as well as outward; and this requirement is fully met by the wondrous and gracious provision which God has made for his people. Here again we may behold the striking and blessed co-operation between the Eternal Three. The Father, as the King and Judge of all, gave the law. The Son, as our Surety, fulfilled the law. The Spirit is given to work in us conformity to the law: first, by imparting a nature which loves it; second,

157

by instructing and giving us a knowledge of its extensive requirements; third, by producing in us strivings after obedience to its precepts. Not only is the perfect obedience of Christ imputed to his people, but a nature which delights in the law is imparted to them. But because of the opposition from indwelling sin, perfect obedience to the law is not possible in this life; yet, for Christ's sake, God accepts their sincere but imperfect obedience.

We must distinguish between the Holy Spirit and the principle of holiness which he imparts at regeneration: the Creator and the nature he creates must not be confounded. It is by his indwelling the Christian that he sustains and develops, continues and perfects, this good work which he has begun in us. He takes possession of the soul to strengthen and direct its faculties. It is from the principle of holiness which he has communicated to us that there proceeds the fruits of holiness – sanctified desires, actions and works. Yet that new principle or nature has no strength of its own: only as it is daily renewed, empowered, controlled, and directed by its Giver, do we act 'as becometh holiness'. His continued work of sanctification within us proceeds in the twofold process of the mortification (subduing) of the old man and the vivification (quickening) of the new man.

The fruit of the Spirit's sanctification of us experimentally appears in our separation from evil and the world. But because of the flesh within, our walk is not perfect. Oftentimes there is little for the eye of sense to distinguish in those in whom the Spirit dwells from the moral and respectable worldlings; yea, often they put us to shame. 'It doth not yet appear what we shall be.' 'The world knoweth us not.' But the heart is washed from the prevailing love of sin by the tears of repentance which the Christian is moved to frequently shed. Every new act of faith upon the cleansing blood of Christ carries forward the work of experimental sanctification to a further degree. As Naaman was required to dip in the Jordan again and again, yea, seven times, till he was wholly purged of his bodily leprosy; so the soul of the Christian – conscious of so much of the filth of sin still defiling him – continues to dip in that 'fountain opened for sin and for uncleanness'. Thank God, one day Christ will 'present to himself a glorious church, not having spot, or wrinkle, or any such thing' (Eph. 5:27).

10

Its Rule

Having considered the distinct acts of the Father, the Son, and the Holy Spirit in the sanctification of the Church, we must now carefully inquire as to the Rule by which all true holiness is determined, the Standard by which it is weighed and to which it must be conformed. This also is of deep importance, for if we mistake the line and plummet of holiness, then all our efforts after it will be wide of the mark. On this aspect of our subject there also prevails widespread ignorance and confusion today, so that we are obliged to proceed slowly and enter rather lengthily into it. If one class of our readers sorely needed – for the strengthening of their faith and the comfort of their hearts – a somewhat full setting forth of the perfect sanctification which believers have in Christ, another class of our readers certainly require – for the illumination of their minds and the searching of their conscience – a setting forth in detail of the Divinely-provided 'Rule'.

In previous chapters we have shown that *holiness is the antithesis of sin*, and therefore as 'sin is the transgression (a deviation from or violation of) the Law' (1 John 3:4), holiness must be *a conformity to the law*. As 'sin' is a general term to connote all that is evil, foul, and morally loathsome, so 'holiness' is a general term to signify all that is good, pure, and morally virtuous or vicious, praiseworthy or blameworthy, as they express the desires, designs, and choices of the heart. As all sin is a species of *self-love* – self-will, self-pleasing, self-gratification – so all holiness consists of disinterested or *unselfish love* – to God and our neighbour: 1 Corinthians 13 supplies a full and beautiful delineation of the nature of holiness: substitute the term 'holiness' for 'love' all through that chapter. As sin is the transgressing of the law, so love is the fulfilling of the law (Rom. 13:10).

The spirituality and religion of man in his original state consisted in a perfect conformity to the divine law, which was the law of his nature (for he was created in the image and likeness of God), with the addition of positive precepts. But when man lost his innocency and became guilty and depraved, he fell not only under the wrath of God, but also under the dominion of sin. Consequently, he now needs both a Redeemer, and *a Sanctifier*; and in the gospel *both* are provided. Alas that so often today only a half gospel, a mutilated gospel, is being preached – whereby sinners are made 'twofold more the children of hell' than they were before they heard it! In the gospel a way is revealed for our obtaining both pardoning mercy and sanctifying grace. The gospel presents Christ not only as a Deliverer from the wrath to come (1 Thess. 1:10), but also as a Sanctifier of his Church (Eph. 5:26).

In his work of sanctifying the Church Christ *restores his people unto a conformity to the law*. Before supplying proof of this statement, let us carefully observe *what it is* which the law required of us. 'Jesus said unto him, Thou shalt love the Lord thy God with all thy heart, and with all thy soul, and with all thy mind. This is the first and great commandment. And the second is like unto it, Thou shalt love thy neighbour as thyself. On these two commandments hang all the Law and the Prophets' (Matt. 22:37-40). Christ here summed up the ten commandments in these two, and *every* duty enjoined by the law and inculcated by the Prophets is but a deduction or amplification of these two, in which *all* are radically contained. Here is, first, the duty required – love to God and our neighbour. Second, the ground or reason of this duty – because he is the Lord *our* God. Third, the measure of this duty – with all the heart.

The grand reason why God, the alone Governor of the world, ever made the law, requiring us to love him with all our hearts, was because it is, in its own nature, infinitely just and fitting. That law is an eternal and unalterable Rule of Righteousness, which cannot be abrogated or altered in the least iota, for it is an unchanging expression of God's immutable moral character. To suppose that he would ever repeal or even abate the law – when the grounds and reasons of God's first making it remain as forcible as ever, when that which it requires is as just and meet as ever, and which it becomes him as the moral Ruler of the universe to require as much as ever – casts the highest reproach upon all his glorious perfections. Such a horrible insinuation could have originated nowhere else than in the foul mind of the Fiend, the arch-enemy of God, and is to be rejected by us with the utmost abhorrence.

To imagine God repealing the moral law, which is the rule of all holiness and the condemner of all sin, would be supposing him to release his creatures from giving unto him the full glory which is his due, and allowing them to hold back a part of it at least. It supposes him releasing his creatures from that which is right and allowing them to do that which is wrong. Yea, such a vile supposition reflects upon God's very goodness, for so far from it being a boon and benefit to his creatures, the repealing or altering this law, which is so perfectly suited to their highest happiness, would be one of the sorest calamities that could happen. If God had rather that heaven and earth should pass away than that the least jot or tittle of the law, should fail

(Matt. 5:18), how steadfastly should we resist every effort of Satan's to rob us of this divine rule, weaken its authority over our hearts, or prejudice us against it.

In the light of what has been pointed out, how unspeakably horrible, that vile blasphemy, to imagine that the Son himself should come from heaven, become incarnate, and die the death of the cross, with the purpose of securing for his people a rescinding or abating of the law, and obtain for them a lawless liberty. What! had he so little regard for his Father's interests and glory, for the honour of his law, that he shed his precious blood so as to persuade the great Governor of the world to slacken the reins of his government and obtain for his people an impious licence? Perish the thought. Let all who love the Lord rise up in righteous indignation against such an atrocious slur upon his holy character, and loathe it as Satanic slander – no matter by whom propagated. Any Spirit-taught reader must surely see that such a wicked idea as the affirming that Christ is the one who has made an end of the law, is to make him the friend of sin and the enemy of God!

Pause for a moment and weigh carefully the implications. How could God possibly vindicate the honour of his great name were he to either repeal or abate that law which requires love to him with all our hearts? Would not this be clearly tantamount to saying that he had previously required more than was his due? Or, to put it in another form, that he does not now desire so much from his creatures as he formerly did? Or, to state the issue yet more baldly: should God now (since the cross) relinquish his *rights* and freely allow his creatures to despise him and sin with impunity? Look at it another way: to what purpose should Christ die in order to secure an abatement from that law? What need was there for it? or what good could it do? If the law *really* demanded too much, then justice required God to make the abatement; in such case the death of Christ was needless.

Or if the law required what *was* right, then God could not in justice make any abatement, and so Christ died in vain!

But so far from Christ coming into this world with any such evil design, he expressly declared: 'Think not that I am come to destroy the Law, or the Prophets; I am not come to destroy, but to fulfil. For verily I say unto you, Till heaven and earth pass, one jot or one tittle shall in no wise pass from the law, till all be fulfilled. Whosoever therefore shall break one of these least commandments, and shall teach men so, he shall be called the least in the kingdom of heaven: but whosoever shall do and teach them, the same shall be called great in the kingdom of heaven' (Matt. 5:17-19). This is the very thing he condemned the Pharisees for all through this chapter. They, in effect, taught this very doctrine, that the law *was* abated, that its exacting demands *were* relaxed. They affirmed that though the law did forbid some external and gross acts of sin, yet it did not reprehend the first stirrings of corruption in the heart or lesser iniquities.

For instance, the Pharisees taught that murder must not be committed, but there was no harm in being angry, speaking reproachfully, or harbouring a secret grudge in the heart (Matt. 5:21-26); that adultery must not be committed, yet there was no evil in having lascivious thoughts (vv. 27-30); that we must not be guilty of perjury, yet there was no harm in petty oaths in common conversation (vv. 33-37); that friends must not be hated, yet it was quite permissible to hate enemies (vv. 43-47). These, and such like allowances, they taught were made in the law, and therefore were not sinful. But such doctrine our Saviour condemned as erroneous and damning, insisting that the law requires us to be as perfect as our heavenly Father is perfect (v. 48), and declaring that if our righteousness exceed not that of the scribes and Pharisees we could not enter the kingdom of heaven (Matt. 5:20). How far, then, was our holy Lord from abating God's law, or lessening our obligations to perfect conformity to it!

165

The fact of the matter is (and here we will proceed to adduce some of the proofs for our statement at the beginning of the fourth paragraph), that Christ came into the world for the express purpose of giving a practical demonstration, in the most public manner, that God is worthy of all that love, honour, and obedience which the law requires, and that sin *is* as great an evil as the punishment of the law implies, and thereby declared God's righteousness and hatred of sin, to the end that God might be just and yet the justifier of every sincere believer. This Christ did by obeying the precepts and suffering the death-penalty of the law in the stead of his people. The great design of the incarnation, life and death of our blessed Lord was to maintain and magnify the divine government, and secure the salvation of his people in a way that placed supreme honour upon the law.

The chief object before the beloved Son in taking upon him the form of a servant was to meet the demands of the law. His work here had a prime respect to the law of God, so that sinners should be justified and sanctified without setting aside its requirements or without showing the least disregard to it. First. he was 'made under the Law' (Gal. 4:4) – amazing place for the Lord of glory to take! Second, he declared, 'Lo, I come: in the volume of the book it is written of me, I delight to do thy will, O my God; yea, thy law is *within my heart*' (Ps. 40:7, 8) – enshrined in his affections. Third, he flawlessly obeyed the commands of the law in thought, and word, and deed: as a Child he was subject to his parents (Luke 2:51); as Man he honoureth the Sabbath (Luke 4:16), and refused to worship or serve any but the Lord his God (Luke 4:8). Fourth, when John demurred at baptising him, he answereth 'Thus it becometh us to fulfil all righteousness' (Matt. 3:15) – what a proof of his *love* for the Lawgiver in submitting to his ordinance! what proof of his *love* for his people in taking his place alongside of them in that which spake of death!

The truth is, that it was God's own infinite aversion to the repeal of the law, as a thing utterly unfit and wrong, which was the very thing which made the death of Christ needful. If the law might have been repealed, then sinners could have been saved without any more ado; but if it must not be repealed, then the demands of it must be answered by some other means, or every sinner would be eternally damned. It was because of this that Christ willingly interposed, and 'magnified the law and made it honourable' (Isa. 42:21), so securing the honour of God's holiness and justice, so establishing his law and government, that a way has been opened for him to pardon the very chief of sinners without compromising himself to the slightest degree. 'As many as are of the works of the law are under the curse ... Christ hath redeemed us from the curse of the law, being made a curse for us' (Gal. 3:10, 13).

Christ loved his *Father's* honour far too much to revoke his law, or bring his people into a state of insubordination to his authority; and he loved *them* too well to turn them adrift from 'the perfect law of liberty'. Read carefully the inspired record of his life upon earth, and you will not discover a single word falling from his lips which expresses the slightest disrespect for the law. Instead we find that he bade his disciples do unto men whatsoever we would that they should do unto us *because* 'this is the Law and the Prophets' (Matt. 7:12). In like manner Christ's apostles urged the performance of moral duties by the authority of the law: 'Owe no man anything, but to love one another: *for* he that loveth another hath fulfilled the Law' (Rom. 13:8); 'Children, obey your parents in the Lord: *for* this is right. Honour thy father and mother; which is the first commandment with promise' (Eph. 6:1, 2). The apostle John exhorted believers to love one another as 'an old commandment which ye had from the beginning' (1 John 2:7). And, as we shall yet show at length, the law is the great means which the Spirit uses in sanctifying us.

Here, then, is a 'threefold cord' which cannot be broken, a threefold consideration which 'settles the matter' for all who submit to the authority of Holy Scripture. First, God the Father honoured the law by refusing to rescind it in order that his people might be saved at less cost, declining to abate its demands even when his own blessed Son cried, 'If it be possible, let this cup pass from Me'. God the Son honoured the law by being made under it, by perfectly obeying its precepts, and by personally enduring its awful penalty. God the Spirit honours the law by making quickened sinners see, feel, and own that it is 'holy, and *just*, and good' (Rom. 7:12) even though it condemns them, and that before ever he reveals the mercy of God through Jesus Christ unto them; so that the law is magnified, sin is embittered, the sinner is humbled, and grace is glorified all at once!

There are some who will go with us this far, agreeing that Christ came here to meet the demands of the law, yet who insist that the law being satisfied, believers are now entirely freed from its claims. But this is the most inconsistent, illogical, absurd position of all. Shall Christ go to so much pains to magnify the law in order that it might now be dishonoured by us! Did he pour out *his* love to God on the cross that we might be relieved from loving him! It is true that 'Christ is the end of the law for righteousness to every one that believeth' (Rom. 10:4) – for 'righteousness' (for our *justification*), yes; but not for our sanctification. Is it not written that 'he that saith he abideth in him ought himself also so to walk, even as he walked' (1 John 2:6), and did not Christ walk according to the rule of the law? The great object in Christ's coming here was to conform his people to the law, and not to make them independent of it. Christ sends the Spirit to write the law in their hearts (Heb. 8:10) and not to set at nought its holy and high demands.

The truth is that God's sending his Son into the world to die for the redemption of his people, instead of freeing them from their obligations to keep the law, binds them the more strongly to do so. This is so obvious that it ought not to require arguing. Reflect for a moment, Christian reader, upon God's dealings with us. We had rebelled against the Lord, lost all esteem for him, cast off his authority, and practically bid defiance to both his justice and his power. What wonder, then, had he immediately doomed our apostate world to the blackness of darkness forever? Instead, he sent forth his own dear Son, his only Begotten, as an Ambassador of peace, with a message of good news, even that of a free and full forgiveness of sins to all who threw down the weapons of their warfare against him, and who took his easy yoke upon them.

But more: when God's Son was despised and rejected of men, he did not recall him to heaven, but allowed him to complete his mission of mercy, by laying down his life as a ransom for all who should believe on him. And now he sends forth his messengers to proclaim the gospel to the ends of the earth, inviting his enemies to cease their rebellion, acknowledge the law by which they stand condemned to be holy, just and good, and to look to him through Jesus Christ for pardon as *a free gift*, and to yield themselves to him entirely, to love him and delight themselves in him forever. Is not this fathomless love, infinite mercy, amazing grace, which should melt our hearts and cause us to 'present our bodies a living sacrifice, holy, acceptable unto God' which is indeed our 'reasonable service' (Rom. 12:1)?

O my Christian reader, that God out of his own mere good pleasure, according to his eternal purpose, should have stopped thee in thy mad career to hell, made thee see and feel thy awful sin and guilt, own the sentence just by which thou wast condemned, and bring thee on thy knees to look for free grace through Jesus Christ for pardon, and through him give up thyself to God forever. And that now he should receive thee to his favour, put thee among his children, become thy Father and thy God, by an everlasting covenant; undertake to teach and guide, nourish and strengthen, correct and comfort, protect and preserve; and while in this world supply all thy need and make all things work together for thy good; and finally bring thee into everlasting glory and blessedness. Does not *this* lay thee under infinitely deeper obligations to *love* the Lord thy God with all thine heart? Does not *this* have the greatest tendency to animate thee unto obedience to his righteous law? Does not *this* engage thee, does not his love constrain thee, to seek to please, honour and glorify him?

Its Rule (2)

We trust it has now been clearly proved to the satisfaction of every *truth-loving* reader that the great object in Christ's coming here was to magnify the law and satisfy its righteous demands. In his fulfilling of the law and by his enduring its penalty, the Lord Jesus laid the foundation for the conforming of his people to it. This is plainly taught us in, 'For what the law could not do (namely, justify and sanctify fallen sinners – neither remit the penalty, nor deliver from the power of sin) in that it was weak through the flesh (unable to produce holiness in a fallen creature, as a master musician cannot produce harmony and melody from an instrument that is all out of tune) God sending his own Son in the likeness of sin's flesh and for sin, condemned sin in the flesh, *that* (in order that) the righteousness of the law (its just requirements) might be *fulfilled in us*' (Rom. 8:3, 4).

This was the design of God in sending his Son here. 'That he would grant unto us, that we, being delivered out of the hand of our enemies, might serve him (be in subjection to him) without fear, in holiness and righteousness before him, all the days of our life' (Luke 1:74, 75). 'Who gave himself for us, that he might redeem us from all iniquity, and purify unto himself a peculiar people, zealous of good works'

(Titus 2:14). 'Who his own self bare our sins in his own body on the tree, that we, being dead to sins, should *live unto righteousness*' (1 Pet. 2:24). These and similar passages, are so many different ways of saying that Christ 'became obedient unto death' in order that his people might be recovered to obedience unto God, that they might be made personally holy, that they might be conformed to God's law, both in heart and life. Nothing less than this would or could meet the requirements of the divine government, satisfy God's own nature, or glorify the Redeemer by a triumphant issue of his costly work.

Nor should it surprise any to hear that nothing short of heart-conformity to the law could satisfy the thrice Holy One. 'The LORD seeth not as man seeth; for man looketh on the outward appearance, but the LORD looketh *on the heart*' (1 Sam. 16:7). We have read the Old Testament Scriptures in vain if we have failed to note what a prominent place this basic and searching truth occupies: any one who has access to a complete Hebrew-English concordance can see at a glance how many *hundreds of* times the term 'heart' is used there. The great God could never be imposed upon or satisfied with mere external performances from his creatures. Alas, alas, that *heart religion* is rapidly disappearing from the earth, to the eternal undoing of all who are strangers to it. God has never required less then the hearts of his creatures: 'My son, give me thine *heart*' (Prov. 23:26).

'Only take heed to thyself, and keep thy *soul* diligently, lest thou forget the things which thine eyes have seen, and lest they depart from thy *heart* all the days of thy life' (Deut. 4:9). 'Circumcise therefore the foreskin of your *heart*, and be no more stiff-necked' (Deut. 10:16, and cf. Jer. 9:25, 26). 'Keep thy *heart* with *all* diligence; for out of it are the issues of life' (Prov. 4:23). 'Therefore also now, saith the LORD, turn ye even to me with all your heart, and with fasting, and with weeping, and with mourning: and *rend your heart* and not your garments, and turn unto the LORD your God: for he is gracious and merciful' (Joel 2:12, 13). The regenerate in Israel clearly *recognized* the high and holy demands which the law of God made upon them: 'Behold, thou desirest truth in the *inward* parts' (Ps. 51:6); and therefore did they pray, 'Search me, O God, and know my *heart*: try me, and know my *thoughts*: and see if there be any wicked way *in* me, and lead me in the way everlasting' (Ps. 139:23, 24).

Now as we pointed out in our last chapter, the Lord Jesus affirmed that the full requirements of the law from us are summed up in, 'Thou shalt *love* the Lord thy God with *all thy heart*, and with all thy soul, and with all thy mind. ...thou shalt *love* thy neighbour as thyself' (Matt. 22:37, 39). It was to restore his people to this that Christ lived and died: to recover them *to God*, to bring them back into subjection *to him* (from which they fell in Adam), to recover them to the Lawgiver. Christ is the Mediator between God and men, and by Christ is the believing sinner brought *to God*. When he sends his ministers to preach the gospel it is 'to open their eyes and to turn them from darkness to light, and from the power of Satan *unto God*' (Acts 26:18). 'All things are of God, who hath reconciled us *to himself* by Jesus Christ' (2 Cor. 5:18). To the saints Paul wrote 'Ye turned *to God* from idols to serve the living and true God' (1 Thess. 1:9). Of Christ it is written 'he is able also to save them to the uttermost that come *unto God* by Him' (Heb. 7:25); and again, 'Christ also hath once suffered for sins, the Just for the unjust, that he might bring us *to God*' (1 Pet. 3:18) – to the God of the Old Testament, the Lawgiver!

Let us now consider *how* Christ recovers his people unto a conformity of the law, *how* he restores them unto the Lawgiver. Since that which the law requires is that we love the Lord our God with all our hearts, it is evident, in the first place, that we must have *a true knowledge of God himself*: this is both requisite unto and implied in the having our affections set unto him. If our apprehensions of God be wrong, if they agree not with the Scriptures, then it is obvious that we have but a false image of him framed by our own fancy. By a true knowledge of God (John 17:3) we mean far more than a correct theoretical notion of his perfections: the demons have *that*, yet they have no *love for* him. Before God can be loved there must be a spiritual knowledge of him, a heartfelt realization of his personal loveliness, moral excellency, ineffable glory.

By nature none of us possess one particle of genuine love for God: so far from it, we *hated* him, though we may not have realized the awful fact, and had we done so, would not have acknowledged it. 'The carnal mind is *enmity* against God, for it is not subject to the law of God, neither indeed can be' (Rom. 8:7): those are equivalents, convertible terms. Where there is enmity toward God, there is in subjection to his law; contrariwise, where there is love for God, there is submission to his law. The reason why there is no love for God in the unregenerate is because they have no real knowledge of him: this is just as true of those in Christendom as it is of those in heathendom – to the highly privileged and well-instructed Jews Christ said, 'Ye neither *know* me, nor my Father' (John 8:19, 55). A miracle of grace has to take place in order to this: 'For God, who commanded the light to shine out of darkness, hath shined in our hearts, *to give* the light of the knowledge of the glory of God in the face of Jesus Christ' (2 Cor. 4:6); 'We know that the Son of God is come, and hath given us an understanding, *that we may* know him that is true' (1 John 5:20).

This true knowledge of God consists in our spiritually perceiving him (in our measure) to be just such an One *as he actually is*. We see him to be not only love itself, the God of all grace and the Father of mercies, but also supreme, infinitely exalted above all creatures; sovereign, doing as he pleases, asking no one's permission and giving no account of his actions; immutable, with whom there is no variableness or shadow of turning; ineffably holy, being of purer eyes than to behold evil and canst not look on iniquity; inflexibly just, so that he will by no means clear the guilty; omniscient, so that no secret can be concealed from him; omnipotent, so that no creature can successfully resist him; the judge of all, who will banish from his presence into everlasting woe and torment every impenitent rebel. This is the character of the true God: do you *love* HIM, my reader?

Second, *a high esteem for God* is both requisite unto and is implied in loving him. This high esteem consists of exalted thoughts and a lofty valuation of him from the sight and sense we have of his own intrinsic worthiness and excellency. To the unregenerate he says, 'Thou thoughtest that I was altogether such an one as thyself' (Ps. 50:21), for their concepts of God are mean, low, derogatory. But when the Spirit quickens us and shines upon our understandings we discern the beauty of the Lord, and admire and adore him. We join with the celestial hosts in exclaiming, 'Holy, holy, holy, is the Lord of hosts'. As we behold, as in a glass, his glory, we see how infinitely exalted he is above all creatures, and cry, 'Who is like unto thee, O LORD, among the gods? who is like thee, glorious in holiness, fearful in praises, doing wonders?' yea, we confess 'Whom have I in heaven but thee? and there is none upon earth that I desire beside Thee' (Ps. 73:25).

Now this high estimate of God not only disposes or inclines the heart to acquiesce, but to *exult* in his high prerogatives. From a consciousness of his own infinite excellency, his entire right thereto, and his absolute authority over all, occupying the throne of the universe, he presents himself as the Most High God, supreme Lord, sovereign Governor of all worlds, and demands that all creatures shall be in a perfect subjection to him; deeming those who refuse him this as worthy of eternal damnation. He declares, 'I am the Lord, and beside me there is no God: my glory will I not give to another: thus and thus shall ye do, because I am THE LORD.' As it would be the utmost wickedness for the highest angel in heaven to assume any of this honour to himself, yet it perfectly becomes the Almighty so to do: yea, so far above all is he, that God is worthy of and entitled to infinitely more honour and homage than all creatures together can possibly pay to him.

When the eyes of our hearts are open to see something of God's sovereign majesty, infinite dignity, supernal glory, and we begin to rightly esteem him, then we perceive how thoroughly right and just it is that such an One *should* be held in the utmost reverence, and esteemed far above all others and exulted in: 'Sing unto the LORD all the earth' (Ps. 96:1). A spiritual sight and sense of the supreme excellency and infinite glory of the Triune Jehovah will not only rejoice our hearts to know that he is King of kings, the Governor of all worlds, but we are also thankful and glad that *we* live under his government, and are *his* subjects and servants. We shall then perceive the grounds and reasons of his law; how infinitely right and fit it is that we *should* love him with all our hearts and obey him in everything; how infinitely unfit and wrong the least sin is, and how just the threatened punishment. We shall then also perceive that all the nations of the earth are but as a drop in the bucket before *him*, and that we ourselves are less than nothing in his sight.

Third, *a deep and lasting desire for God's glory* is both requisite unto and is implied in our loving him. When we are acquainted with a person who appears very excellent in our eyes and we highly esteem him, then we heartily wish him well and are ready at all times to do whatever we can to promote his welfare. It is thus that love to God will make us feel and act toward *his* honour and interests in this world. When God is spiritually beheld in his infinite excellency, as the sovereign Governor of the whole world, and a sense of his infinite worthiness is alive in our hearts, a holy benevolence is enkindled, the spontaneous language of which is, 'Give unto the LORD, O ye kindreds of the people, give unto the LORD glory and strength: give unto the LORD the glory due unto his name' (Ps. 96:7, 8). 'Be thou exalted, O God, above the heavens; let thy glory be above all the earth' (Ps. 57:5). As self-love naturally causes us to seek the promotion of our *own* interests and self-aggrandizement, so a true love to God moves us to put him first and seek his glory.

This holy disposition expresses itself in earnest longings that God would glorify himself and honour his great name by bringing more of our fellow-creatures into an entire subjection to himself. The natural longing and language of true spiritual love is, 'Our Father which art in heaven, Hallowed be thy name; thy kingdom come; thy will be done on earth as it is in heaven.' When God is about to bring to pass great and glorious things to the magnifying of himself, it causes great rejoicing: 'Let the heavens rejoice, and let the earth be glad.... He shall judge the world with righteousness, and the people with his truth' (Ps. 96:11, 13). So too when God permits anything which, as it seems to us, tends to bring reproach and dishonour upon his cause, it occasions acute anguish and distress: as when the Lord threatened to destroy Israel for their stiff-neckedness, Moses exclaimed 'What will become of *thy* great name? what will the *Egyptians* say!'

From this disinterested affection arises a free and genuine disposition to give ourselves entirely to the Lord forever, to walk in his ways and keep all his commandments, For if we really desire that God may be glorified, *we* shall be disposed to *seek* his glory. A spiritual sight and sense of the infinite greatness, majesty, and excellency of the Lord of ords, makes it appear to us supremely fit that we should be wholly devoted to him, and that it is utterly wrong for us to live to ourselves and make our own interests our last end. The same desire which makes the godly earnestly long to have God glorify himself, strongly prompts them to live unto him. If we love God with all our hearts, we shall serve him with all our strength. If God be the highest in our esteem, then his honour and glory will be our chief concern. To love God so as to *serve him* is what the law requires; to love self so as to *serve it*, is rebellion against the Majesty of heaven.

Fourth, *delighting ourselves in God* is both requisite unto and is implied in our loving him. If there be a heartfelt realization of God's personal loveliness and ineffable glory, then the whole soul must and will be attracted to him. A spiritual sight and sense of the perfections of the divine character draw out the heart in fervent adoration. When we 'delight in' a fellow-creature, we find pleasure and satisfaction in his company and conversation; we long to see him when absent, rejoice in his presence, and the enjoyment of him makes us happy. So it is when a holy soul beholds God in the grandeur of his being, loves him above all else, and is devoted to him entirely – *now* he delights in him supremely. His delight and complacency is as great as his esteem, arising from the same sense of God's moral excellency.

From this delight in God springs longings after a fuller acquaintance and closer communion with him: 'O God, thou art my God; early will I seek thee: my soul thirsteth for thee, my flesh longeth for thee in a dry and thirsty land, where no water is: to see thy power and thy glory ... because thy lovingkindness is better than life ... my soul followeth hard after thee' (Ps. 63:1-8). There is at times a holy rejoicing in God which nothing can dim: 'Although the fig tree shall not blossom, neither shall fruit be in the vines; the labour of the olive shall fail, and the fields shall yield no meat; the floc shall be cut off from the fold, and there shall be no herd i the stalls: YET I will *rejoice in the* LORD, I will joy in the Go of my salvation' (Hab. 3:17, 18). From this delight in Go arises a holy disposition to renounce all others and to liv wholly upon him, finding our satisfaction in him alone: 'C LORD our God, other lords besides thee *have had* dominio over us: but by thee only *will we* make mention of thy name (Isa. 26:13); 'I count all things but loss for the excellency o the knowledge of Christ Jesus my Lord: for whom I hav suffered the loss of all things, and do count them but dung that I may win Christ' (Phil. 3:8). As the proud man seek contentment in creature honours, the worldling in riches the Pharisee in his round of duties, so the true lover of Go finds his contentment in God himself.

That these four things are a true representation of th nature of that love which is required in the first and grea commandment of the law, upon which chiefly hang al the Law and the Prophets, is manifest, not only from th reason of things, but from this: that *such* a love lays a sur and firm foundation for all holy *obedience*. Only that lov to God is of the right kind which effectually influences u: to keep his commandments: 'Hereby we do know that w know him, if we keep his commandments. He that saith, know him, and keepeth not his commandments, is a liar and the truth is not in him. But whoso keepeth his Word in him verily is the love of God perfected' (1 John 2:3-5) But it is evident from the very nature of things that sucl a love as this *will* effectually influence us so to do. As self love naturally moves us to set up self and its interests, sc *this* love will move us to set up God and his interests. The only difference between the love of saints in heaven and o saints on earth is one of *degree*.

Having shown that the great object in Christ's coming to earth was to magnify the law (by obeying its precept:

nd suffering its penalty), and that by so doing he laid a oundation for the recovering of his people to the Lawgiver, t now remains for us to consider more specifically *how* he conforms them to the law. This, as we have just seen, must consist in his bringing them to lay down the weapons of their warfare against God, and by causing them to love God with all their heart. This he accomplishes by *the sending forth of his blessed Spirit to renew them*, for 'the love of God is shed abroad in our hearts by the Holy Spirit which is given unto us' (Rom. 5:5). It is the special and supernatural work of the Spirit in the soul which distinguishes the regenerate from the unregenerate.

Previously we have shown at length that the regenerating and sanctifying work of the Spirit is an orderly and progressive one, conducting the soul step by step in the due method of the gospel: quickening, illuminating, convicting, drawing to Christ, and cleansing. That order can be best perceived by us inversely, according as it is realized in our conscious experience, tracing it backward from effect to cause.

(5) Without the Spirit bringing us to Christ there can be no cleansing from his blood.

(4) Without the Spirit working in us evangelical repentance there can be no saving faith or coming to Christ.

(3) Without divine conviction of sin there can be no godly sorrow for it.

(2) Without the Spirit's special illumination there can be no sight or sense of the exceeding sinfulness of sin, wherein it consists – opposition to God, expressed in self-pleasing.

(1) Without his quickening us we can neither see nor feel our dreadful state before God: spiritual life must be imparted before we are capable of discerning or being affected by divine things.

It is by the Spirit we are brought from death unto life, given spiritual perception to realize our utter lack of conformity to the divine law, enabled to discern it spirituality and just requirements, brought to mourn ove our fearful transgressions against it and to acknowledge th justice of its condemning sentence upon us. It is by the Spir we receive a new nature which loves God and delights i his law, which brings our hearts into conformity to it. Th *extent* of this conformity in the *present* life, and the harassin; difficulty presented to the Christian by the realization tha there is still so much in him which is *opposed* to the law must be left for consideration in our next chapter.

Its Rule (3)

It has been pointed out in earlier chapters that our practica sanctification by the Spirit is but his continuing and completing of the work which he began in us at regeneratior and conversion. Now saving conversion consists in ou being delivered from our depravity and sinfulness to the moral image of God, or, which is the same thing, to a rea conformity unto the moral law. And a conformity to the moral law (as we showed in our last chapter) consists in a *disposition* to love God supremely, live to him ultimately and delight in him superlatively; and to love our neighbour as ourselves, with a *practice* agreeing thereto. Therefore a saving conversion consists in our being recovered from what we are by nature *to such* a disposition and practice.

In order to this blessed recovery of us to God, Christ by his Spirit applies the law in power to the sinner's understanding and heart, for 'the law of the LORD is perfect converting the soul' (Ps. 19:7). That effectual application or the law causes the sinner to see clearly and to feel acutely *how* he had lived – in utter defiance of it; *what* he is – a fou leper; what he *deserves* – eternal punishment; and how he is in the hands of a sovereign God, entirely at *his disposal* (see Rom. 9:18). This experience is unerringly described in, 'For without (the Spirit's application of) the law, sin was dead (we had no perception or feeling of its heinousness). 'or I was alive without the law once (deeming myself as good as anyone else, and able to win God's approval by my religious performances): but when the commandment came (in power to my conscience), sin revived (became a fearful reality as I discovered the plague of my heart), and died' (to my self-righteousness) – Romans 7:8, 9.

It is then, for the first time, that the soul perceives 'the law is *spiritual*' (Rom. 7:14), that it requires not only outward works of piety, but holy thoughts and godly affections, from whence all good works must proceed, or else they are unacceptable to God. The law is 'exceeding broad' (Ps. 119:96), taking notice not only of our outward conduct but also of our inward state; 'love' is its demand, and *that* is essentially a thing of the *heart*. As the law requires love, and nothing but love (to God and our neighbour), so all sin consists in that which is contrary to what the law requires, and therefore every exercise of the heart which is not agreeable to the law, which is not prompted by holy love, is opposed to it and is *sinful*. Therefore did Christ plainly declare, 'Whosoever looketh on a woman to lust after her hath committed adultery with her already in his heart' (Matt. 5:28).

God requires far more than a correct outward deportment: 'Behold, thou desirest truth in the *inward* parts' (Ps. 51:6). The law takes cognizance of the thoughts and intents of the heart, saying, 'thou shalt not *covet*', which is an act of the soul rather than of the body. When a sinner is brought to realize *what* the high and holy demands of the law really are, and how utterly he has failed to meet them, he begins to perceive something of the awfulness of his condition, for 'by the law is the knowledge of sin' (Rom. 3:20). Now it is that the awakened sinner realizes how justly the law condemns and curses him as an inveterate and excuseless transgressor of it. Now it is that he has a lively sense in his own soul of the dreadfulness of eternal damnation. Now it is he discovers that he is *lost*, utterly and hopelessly lost so far as any self-help is concerned.

This it is which prepares him to see his dire need of Christ, for they that are whole (in their self-complacency and self-righteousness), betake not themselves to the great Physician. Thus the law (in the hands of the Spirit) is the handmaid of the gospel. Was not this the divine order even at Sinai? The moral law was given first, and then the ceremonial law, with its priesthood and sacrifices: the one to convict of Israel's need of a Saviour, the other setting forth the Saviour under various types and figures! It is not until sin 'abounds' in the stricken conscience of the Spirit convicted transgressor, that grace will 'much more abound' in the estimation and appreciation of his Spirit-opened heart. In exact proportion as we really perceive the justice dignity, and excellency of the law, will be our realization of the infinite evil of sin; and in exact proportion to our sense of the exceeding sinfulness of sin will be our wonderment at the riches of divine grace.

Then it is that 'God, who commanded the light to shine out of darkness, shines in our hearts, unto the light of the knowledge of the glory of God in the face of Jesus Christ' (2 Cor. 4:6). As an experimental sense of the glory of God's *righteousness* in the law and of his *grace* in the gospel is imparted to the soul by the Spirit, the sinner is moved to return home to God, through the Mediator, to venture his soul and its eternal concerns upon his free grace, and to give up himself to be *his* forever – to love him supremely, live to him entirely, and delight in him superlatively. Hereby his heart begins to be habitually framed to love his neighbour as himself, with a disinterested impartiality; and thus an effectual foundation is laid in his heart for universal external obedience, for nothing but a spontaneous and *cheerful* obedience can be acceptable to God, an obedience

hich flows from love and gratitude, an obedience which is
ndered without repining or grudging, as though it were
grievous burden to us.

It is thus that Christ, by his Spirit, conforms us to God's
w. First, by enlightening our understandings, so that
e perceive the spirituality of the law, in its high and
eet demands upon our hearts. Second, by bringing us
) perceive the holiness and justice of its requirements.
hird, by convicting us of our lifelong trampling of the law
eneath our feet. Fourth, by causing us to mourn over our
icked defiance of its authority. And fifth, by imparting
) us a new nature or principle of holiness. Now it is that
e Lord puts his laws into our minds and writes them in
ur hearts (Heb. 8:10). Thus, so far from the grace of the
ospel 'making void the Law', it *establishes* it (Rom. 3:31)
ι our consciences and affections. A spiritual and universal
bedience is what the law demands.

The principal duties of love to God above all, and to
ur neighbours for his sake, are not only required by the
overeign will of God, but are in their own nature 'holy,
ıst and good' (Rom. 7:12), and therefore meet for us to
erform. These are the two main roots from which issue all
ther spiritual fruits, and apart from them there can be no
oliness of heart and life. And the powerful and effectual
neans by which this end is attained is the grand work of
he Spirit in *sanctifying* us, for by *that* our hearts and lives
re conformed to the law. He must bestow upon us an
nclination and disposition of heart *to* the duties of the law,
o as to fit and enable us unto the practice of them. For these
luties are of such a nature as cannot possibly be performed
vhile we have a disinclination for them.

As the divine life is thus begun, so it is *carried* on in the
oul much after the same order. The Spirit of God shows
he believer, more and more, what a sinful, worthless,
ıell-deserving wretch he is in himself, and so makes him

increasingly sensible of his imperative need of free grace through Jesus Christ, to pardon and sanctify him. He has an ever-deepening sense of those two things all his days, and thereby his heart is kept humble, and Christ and free grace made increasingly precious. The Spirit of God shows the believer more and more the infinite glory and excellence of God, whereby he is influenced to love him, live to him, and delight in him with all his heart; and thereby his heart is framed more and more to love his neighbour as himself. Thus 'the path of the just is as the shining light, that shineth *more and more* unto the perfect day' (Prov. 4:18).

The last paragraph needs the following qualifications: the Spirit's operations *after* conversion are attended with two differences, arising from two causes. First, the *different state* the subject is in. The believer, being no longer under the law as a covenant, is not, by the Spirit, filled with those legal *terrors* arising from the fears of hell, as he formerly was (Rom. 8:15); rather is he now made increasingly sensible of his *corruptions*, of the sinfulness of sin, of his base ingratitude against such a gracious God; and hereby his heart is broken. Second, from *the different nature* of the subject wrought upon. The believer, no longer being under the full power of sin nor completely at enmity against God, does not resist the Spirit's operation as he once did, but has a genuine disposition to join with him against sin in himself, saying, Lord, correct, chasten me, do with me as thou wilt, only subdue my iniquities and conform me more and more unto thy image.

A few words now upon *the relation of the gospel*. First, the grace of the gospel is not granted to counterbalance the rigour of the law, or to render God's plan of government justifiable so as to sweeten the minds of his embittered enemies. The law is 'holy, just and good' in itself, and was so before Christ became incarnate. God is not a tyrant nor did his Son die a sacrifice to tyranny, to recover his njured people from the severity of a cruel law. It is utterly mpossible that the Son of God should die to answer the lemands of an unrighteous law. Second, the law, as it is applied by the Spirit, prepares the heart for the gospel: he one giving me a real knowledge of sin, the other revealing how I may obtain deliverance from its guilt and power. Third, *the law*, and not the gospel, is the rule of our sanctification: the one makes known what it is that God requires from me, the other supplies means and motives or complying therewith.

Fourth, the law and the gospel are not in opposition, but in apposition, the one being the handmaid of the other: they exist and work simultaneously and harmoniously in the experience of the believer. Fifth, the high and holy demands of the law are *not* modified to the slightest degree by the gospel: 'Be ye therefore perfect, even as your Father which is in heaven is perfect' (Matt. 5:48); 'But as he which hath called you is holy, so be ye holy in all manner of conversation' (1 Pet. 1:15) is *the standard* set before us. Sixth, thus the Christian's rule of righteousness is the law, but in the hands of the mediator; 'Being not without law to God, but under the law to Christ' (1 Cor. 9:21) – beautifully typed out in the law being given to Israel at Sinai after their redemption from Egypt, through Moses *the typical Mediator* (Gal. 3:19). Seventh, herein we may see the seriousness of the God-dishonouring error of all those who repudiate the moral law as the Christian's rule of life.

'The holy law of God and the gospel of his grace reflect the divine glory, the one upon the other reciprocally, and both will shine forth with joint glory eternally in heaven. The law setting forth, in the brightest light, the beauty of holiness, and the vileness and fearful demerit of sin, will show the abounding grace that hath brought the children of wrath thither, with infinite lustre and glory; and Grace will do honour to the law, by showing in sinners, formerly very vile and polluted, the purity and holiness of the law fully exemplified in their

> perfect sanctification; and Christ, the Lamb that was slain, by
> whom the interests of the law and of Grace have been hap-
> pily reconciled and inseparably united, will be glorified in his
> saints and admired by them who believe' (James Fraser, *The
> Scriptural Doctrine of Sanctification*, 1760).

It is, then, by the regenerating and sanctifying work of
his Spirit that Christ brings his people to a conformity
unto the law and to a compliance with the gospel. 'But
we all, with open face beholding as in a glass the glory of
the Lord, are changed into the same image from glory to
glory, by the Spirit of the Lord' (2 Cor. 3:18). The 'glory
of the Lord' is beheld by us, first, as it shines in the glass
of the law – the glory of his justice and holiness, the glory
of his governmental majesty and authority, the glory of
his goodness in framing such a law, which requires that
we love him with all our hearts, and, for his sake, as *his*
creatures, our neighbours as ourselves. The 'glory of the
Lord' is beheld by us, second, as it shines forth in the glass
of the gospel – the glory of his redeeming love, the glory of
his amazing grace, the glory of his abounding mercy. And,
as renewed creatures, beholding this, we are '*changed* (the
Greek word is the same as Christ being 'transfigured') *into
the same image*, from glory to glory (progressively, from
one degree of it to another) by the Spirit of the Lord': that
is, into a real conformity to the law, and a real compliance
with the gospel.

The gospel calls upon us to *repent*, but there can be no
genuine repentance until we see and feel ourselves to be
guilty transgressors of the law, and until we are brought
by the Spirit to realize that *we* are *wholly* to blame for not
having lived in perfect conformity to it. Then it is we clearly
realize that we thoroughly deserve to be damned, and that
notwithstanding all our doings and religious performances.
Yea, then it is that we perceive that all our previous religious
performances were done not from any love for God, or

with any real concern for his glory, but formally and hypocritically, out of self-love, from fear of hell, and with mercenary hope of gaining heaven thereby. Then it is that our mouth is stopped, all excuses and extenuations silenced, and the curse of the law upon us is acknowledged as just. Then it is that seeing God to be so lovely and glorious a Being, we are stricken to the heart for our vile enmity against him, and condemn ourselves as incorrigible wretches. *Such* are some of the elements of *genuine* repentance.

The gospel calls upon us to *believe*, to receive upon divine authority its amazing good news: that a grievously insulted God has designs of mercy upon his enemies; that the Governor of the world, whose law has been so flagrantly, persistently, and awfully trampled upon by us, has, in his infinite wisdom, devised a way whereby we can be pardoned, without his holy law being dishonoured or its righteous claims set aside; that such is his wondrous love for us that he gave his only begotten Son to be made under the law, to personally and perfectly keep its precepts, and then endure its awful penalty and die beneath its fearful curse. But when a sinner has been awakened and quickened by the Holy Spirit, *such* a revelation of pure grace seems 'too good to be true'. To him it appears that *his* case is utterly hopeless, that he has transgressed beyond the reach of mercy, that he has committed the unpardonable sin. One in *this* state (and we sincerely pity the reader if he or she has never passed through it) can no more receive the gospel into his heart than he can create a world. Only the Holy Spirit can bestow saving faith.

The gospel calls upon us to *obey*, to surrender ourselves fully to the Lordship of Christ, to take his yoke upon us, to walk even as he walked. Now the yoke which Christ wore was unreserved submission to the will of God, and the rule by which he walked was being regulated in all things by the divine law. Therefore does Christ declare, 'If any man will come after me, let him deny himself, and take up his cross and follow me' (Matt. 16:24), for he has left us an example that we should follow his steps. It is their refusal to comply with this demand of the gospel which seals the doom of all who disregard its claims. As it is written, 'The Lord Jesus shall be revealed from heaven with his mighty angels, in flaming fire taking vengeance on them that know not God and that *obey not* the Gospel' (2 Thess. 1:7, 8); and again 'For the time is come that judgment must begin at the house of God:; and if it first begin at us, what shall the end be of them that *obey not* the gospel of God!' (1 Pet. 4:17). But such obedience as the gospel requires can only be rendered by the sanctifying operations of the gracious Holy Spirit.

Marvellous indeed is the change which the poor sinner passes through under the regenerating and converting operations of the Spirit in his soul: he is made a new creature in Christ, and is brought into quite new circumstances. Perhaps the closest analogy to it may be found in the experience of orphan children, left without any guardian or guide, running wild and indulging themselves in all folly and riot; then being taken into the family of a wise and good man and adopted as his children. These lawless waifs are brought into new surroundings and influences: love's care for them wins their hearts, new principles are instilled into their minds, a new temper is theirs, and a new discipline regulates them; old things have passed away, all things have become new to them. So it is with the Christian: from being without God and hope in the world, from running to eternal ruin, they are delivered from the power of darkness and brought into the kingdom of Christ. A new nature has been communicated to them, the Spirit himself indwells them, and a reconciled God now bestows upon them a Father's care, feeding, guiding, protecting them, and ultimately conducting them into everlasting glory.

ts Rule (Completed)

The unchanging moral law of God, which requires us to ove him with all our hearts and our neighbours as ourselves, s the believer's rule of life, the standard of holiness to which is character and conduct must be conformed, the line and olummet by which his internal desires and thoughts as well is outward deeds are measured. And, as has been shown, ve are conformed to that law by the sanctifying operations of the Holy Spirit. This he does by making us see and feel he heinousness of all sin, by delivering us from its reigning oower, and by communicating to us an inclination and disposition of heart *unto* the requirements of the law, so hat we are thereby fitted and enabled to the practice of obedience. While enmity against God reigns within – as it does in every unregenerate soul – it is impossible for love o give that obedience which the law demands.

We concluded our last chapter by showing something of he marvellous and radical change which a sinner passes hrough when he is truly converted to God. One who has really surrendered to the claims of God *approves* of his law: I love thy commandments above gold; yea, above fine gold. Therefore I esteem all thy precepts concerning all things to be right; and I hate every false way' (Ps. 119:127, 128). And why do not the unregenerate do likewise? Because they have no love for a holy God. But believers, loving a holy God in Christ, must love the law also, since in it the image of his holiness is displayed. The converted have a real inclination of heart unto *the whole* law: 'The law of thy mouth is better unto me than thousands of gold and silver ... *all* thy commandments are faithful' (Ps. 119:72, 86). There is in the regenerate a fixed principle which lies the same way as the holy law, bending away from what the law forbids and toward what it enjoins.

The converted habitually *endeavour* to *conform* their outward conduct to the whole law: 'O that my ways

189

were directed to keep thy statutes! Then shall I not be ashamed, when I have respect unto all thy commandments (Ps. 119:5, 6). They desire a *fuller knowledge* of and obedience to the law: 'Teach me, O LORD, the way of thy statutes; and I shall keep it unto the end. Give me understanding, and I shall keep thy law; yea, I shall observe it with my whole heart. Make me to go in the path of thy commandments for therein do I delight' (Ps. 119:33-35). Should any object that these quotations are all made from the *Old* Testament (waiving now the fact that such an objection is quite pointless, for regeneration and its effects, conversion and its fruits, are the same in *all* ages), we would point out that the apostle Paul described his own experience in identically the same terms: 'I delight in the law of God after the inward man ... with the mind I myself serve the law of God' (Rom. 7:22, 25). Thus Christ conforms his people to the law by causing his Spirit to work in them an inclination toward it, a love for it, and an obedience to it.

But at this point a very real and serious difficulty is presented to the believer, for a genuine Christian has an *honest* heart, and detests lies and hypocrisy. That difficulty may be stated thus: If conversion consists in a real conformity to the holiness of God's law, with submission and obedience to its authority, accompanied by a sincere and constant purpose of heart, with habitual endeavour in actual practice, then I dare not regard myself as one who is genuinely converted, for I cannot honestly say that such is *my* experience; nay, I have to sorrowfully and shamefacedly lament that very much in my case is the exact reverse. So far from the reigning power of sin being broken in me, I find my corruptions and lusts raging more fiercely than ever, while my heart is a cage of all unclean things.

The above language will accurately express the feelings of many a trembling heart. As the preceding chapters upon the Rule of our sanctification have been thoughtfully ondered, not a few, we doubt not, are seriously disturbed in their minds. On the one hand, they cannot gainsay what has been written, for they both see and feel that it is according to the Truth; but on the other hand, it *condemns* them, it makes them realize how far, far short they come of measuring up to such a standard; yea, it plainly appears to them that they do not in any sense or to any degree measure up to it at all. Conscious of so much in them that is opposed to the law, conscious of their lack of conformity to it, both inwards and outwards, they bitterly bewail themselves, and cry, 'O wretched man that I am' (Rom. 7:24).

Our first reply is, Thank God for such an honest confession, for it supplies clear evidence that you *are* truly converted. No hypocrite – except it be in the hour of death – ever cries 'O wretched man that I am'. No unregenerate soul ever mourns over his lack of conformity to God's law! Such godly sorrow, dear Christian reader, will enable you to appropriate at least one verse of Scripture to your own case: 'My tears have been my meat day and night' (Ps. 42:3), and those words proceeded not from the bitter remorse of a Judas, but were the utterance of one who had exclaimed 'As the hart panteth after the water brooks, so panteth my soul after thee, O God' (Ps. 42:1). Alas that so many today are ignorant of what constitutes the actual experience of a Christian: defeat as well as victory, grief as well as joy.

Whilst it be a fact that at regeneration a new nature is imparted to us by the Holy Spirit, a nature which is inclined toward and loves the law, it is also a fact that the old nature is *not* removed, nor its opposition to and hatred of the law changed. Whilst it be a fact that a supernatural principle of holiness is communicated to us by the Spirit, it is also a fact that the principle and root of indwelling sin remains, being neither eradicated nor sublimated. The Christian has in him two opposing principles, which produce in him a state of constant warfare: 'For the flesh lusteth against the spirit, an the spirit against the flesh: and these are contrary the on to the other; so that ye cannot do the things that ye would (Gal. 5:17). That 'cannot' looks *both* ways: because of th restraining presence of the 'spirit', the 'flesh' is prevente from fully gratifying its evil desires; and because of th hindering presence of the 'flesh', the 'spirit' is unable t fully realize its aspirations.

It is the presence of and the warfare between these tw natures, the 'flesh' and the 'spirit', the principles of si and holiness, which explain the bewildering state anc conflicting experience of the real Christian; and it is onl as he traces more fully the teaching of Holy Scripture anc carefully compares himself therewith, that light is cas upon what is so puzzling and staggering in his experience Particularly it is in the seventh of Romans that we have the clearest and most complete description of the dual history o a converted soul. Therein we find the apostle Paul, as movec by the Spirit, portraying most vividly and intimately hi own spiritual biography. There are few chapters in the New Testament which the devil hates more than Romans 7, an strenuously and subtly does he strive to rob the Christiar of its comforting and establishing message.

As we have shown above, the Christian approves of the law, and owns it to be 'holy, and just, and good' (Rom. 7:12). He does so, even though the law *condemns* many things in him, yea condemns all in him which is unholy and ungodly. But more: the Christian *condemns himself* – 'For that which I do I *allow not*: for what I would, that do I not; but what I hate, that do I' (Rom. 7:15). So far from sin affording him satisfaction, it is the Christian's greatest grief. The more he perceives the excellency of God and what he is entitled to from his creatures, and the more he realizes what a debtor he is to divine grace and the loving obedience he ought to render out of gratitude, the more acute is the Christian's sorrow for his sad and continual failures to be what he ought to be and to live as he should.

Our second answer to one who is deeply distressed over the raging of his lusts and fears that he has never been soundly converted, is this: the fact is, that the more holy a person is, and the more his heart is truly sanctified, the more clearly does he perceive his corruptions and the more painfully does he feel the plague of his heart; while he utters his complaints in strong expressions and with bitterness of soul. In God's light we see light! It is not that sin has greater control of us than formerly, but that we now have *eyes to see* its fearful workings, and our consciences are *more sensitive* to feel its guilt. An unregenerate person is like a sow wallowing in the mire: his impurities and iniquities afford him satisfaction, and give him little or no concern, no, not even the unholiness of his outward practice, much less the unholiness of his heart.

There is a notable difference between the sensibilities and expressions of the unconverted and the converted. An unregenerate person, who indulges freely in a course of evil practice, will nevertheless give a *favourable* account of himself: he will boast of his good-heartedness, his kindness, his generosity, his praiseworthy qualities and good deeds. On the other hand, persons truly holy, even when kept pure in their outward behaviour, yet conscious of their indwelling corruptions, will *condemn* themselves in unsparing language. The unholy fix their attention on anything good they can find in themselves, and this renders them easy in an evil course. But a truly sanctified person is ready to overlook his spiritual attainments and fruits, and fixes his attention, with painful consciousness, on those respects in which he *lacks* conformity to Christ.

A Christian will say, I thought I had tasted that the Lord is gracious and that my heart had undergone a happy change, with a powerful determination toward God and holiness.

I concluded I had some sound evidence of true conversion and of a heart that was really regenerated. Yet I knew the effect should be to grow in grace, to advance in holiness, and to be more delivered from sin. But alas, I find it quite otherwise. If there is grace in me, it is becoming weaker, and even though my outward conduct be regulated by the precepts of the law, yet in my heart sin is becoming stronger and stronger – evil lusts, carnal affections, worldly desires, and disorderly passions, are daily stirring, often with great vehemence, defiling my spirit. Alas, after all, I fear my past experience was only a delusion, and the dread of the final outcome often strikes terror throughout my whole soul.

Dear friend, it is true that there is much in every Christian which affords great cause for self-judgment and deep humbling of ourselves before God; yet this is a very different matter from sin obtaining fuller dominion over us. Where sin gains power, there is always a corresponding *hardening* of heart and spiritual *insensibility*. Sin is served *willingly* by the wicked, and is sweet and pleasant to them. But if *you* sorrow over sin, sincerely and vigorously oppose it, condemn yourself for it, then old things have passed away and all is become new.

> 'Christians may be assured that a growing sensibility of con-science and heart sorrow for sin is among the chief evidences of growth in grace and of good advances in holiness that they are likely to have on this side of heaven. For the more pure and holy the heart is, it will naturally have the more quick feeling of whatever sin remaineth in it' (James Fraser).

The *dual* experience of the Christian is plainly intimated in Paul's statement: 'So then with the mind I myself serve the law of God; but with the flesh the law of sin' (Rom. 7:25). But some one may reply, the opening verse of the next chapter says, 'There is therefore now no condemnation to them which are in Christ Jesus, who *walk not after the flesh*, but after the Spirit.' Ah, note the minute accuracy of

Scripture: had it said, 'who *act not according* to the flesh' we might well despair, and conclude for a certainty we were not Christians at all. But 'walking' is a *deliberate* course, in which a man proceeds *freely*, without force or struggle; it is the reverse of his being dragged or driven. But when the believer follows the dictates of the flesh, it is *against* the holy desires of his heart, and with reluctance to the new nature! But does not Romans 8:4 affirm, that Christ died in order that 'the righteousness of the law might be fulfilled in us'? Again we answer, admire the marvellous accuracy of Scripture; it does *not* say, 'the righteousness of the law is *now* fulfilled in us'. It is not so, perfectly, in this life, but it will be so at our glorification.

Perhaps the reader is inclined to ask, But *why* does God suffer the sinful nature to remain in the Christian: he could easily remove it. Beware, my friend, of calling into question God's infinite wisdom: he knows what is best, and *his* thoughts and ways are often the opposite of ours (Isa. 55:8). But let me ask, *Which* magnifies God's *power* the more: to preserve in this wicked world one who still has within him a corrupt nature, or one that has been made as sinless as the holy angels? Can there be any doubt as to the answer! But why does not God *subdue* my lusts: Would it not be more for his glory if he did? Again, we say, Beware of measuring God with *your* mind. He knows which is most for his glory. But answer this question: If your lusts *were* greatly subdued and you sinned far less than you do, would you appreciate and adore his *grace* as you now do?

Our third answer to the deeply exercised soul who calls into question the genuineness of his conversion, is this: Honestly apply to yourself the following tests. First, in seasons of retirement from the noise and business of the world, or during the secret hours of the Sabbath, or in your secret devotions, *what* are your thoughts, what is the real temper of your mind? Do you *know* God, commune with and delight in him? Is his Word precious, is prayer a welcome exercise? Do you delight in God's perfections and esteem him for his absolute supremacy and sovereignty? Do you feel and lament your remaining blindness and ignorance, do you mourn over your lack of conformity to God's law and your natural contrariety to it, and hate yourself for it? Do you watch and pray and fight against the corruption of your heart? Not indeed as you *should*, but do you really and sincerely do so at all?

Second, what are the *grounds* of your love to God? from what motives are you influenced to love him? Because you believe he loves you? or because he appears infinitely great and glorious in himself? Are you glad that he *is* infinitely holy, that he knows and sees all things, that he possesses all power? Does it suit your heart that God governs the world, and requires that all creatures should bow in the dust before him, that he alone may be exalted? Does it appear perfectly reasonable that you should love God with all your heart, and do you loathe and resist everything contrary to him? Do you feel yourself to be wholly to blame for not being altogether such as the law requires? Third, is there being formed within you a disposition to love your neighbour as yourself, so that you wish and seek only his good? and do you hate and mourn over any contrary spirit within you? Honest answers to these questions should enable you to ascertain your real spiritual state.

> 'The holiness which the gospel requireth will *not* be maintained either in the hearts or lives of men *without a continual conflict*, warring, contending; and that with all diligence, watchfulness, and perseverance therein. It is our *warfare*, and the Scripture abounds in the discovery of the adversaries we have to conflict withal, their power and subtlety, as also in directions and encouragements unto their resistance. To suppose that gospel obedience will be kept up in our hearts and lives without a continual management of a vigorous warfare against its enemies, is to deny the Scripture and the experi-

ence of all that believe and obey God in sincerity. Satan, sin and the world, are continually assaulting of it, and seeking to ruin its interest in us. The devil will not be resisted, which it is our duty to do (1 Pet. 5:8, 9) without a sharp contest; in the management whereof we are commanded to "take unto ourselves the whole armour of God" (Eph. 6:13). Fleshly lusts do continually war against our souls (1 Pet. 2:11), and if we maintain not a warfare unto the end against them, they will be our ruin. Nor will the power of the world be any otherwise avoided than by a victory over it (1 John 5:4), which will not be carried without contending.

'But I suppose it needs no great confirmation unto any who know what it is to serve and obey God in temptations, that the life of faith and race of holiness will *not* be persevered in *without a severe striving*, labouring, contending, with diligence and persistence; so that I shall take it as a principle (notionally at least) agreed upon by the generality of Christians. If we like not to be holy on *these* terms, we must let it alone, for on any other we shall never be so. If we faint in *this* course, if we give it over, if we think what we aim at herein not to be worth the obtaining or persevering by such a severe contention all our days, we must be content to be without it. Nothing doth so promote the interest of hell and destruction in the world, as a presumption that a lazy slothful performance of some duties and an abstinence from some sins, is that which God will accept of as our obedience. Crucifying of sin, mortifying our inordinate affections, contesting against the whole interest of the flesh, Satan, and the world, and that in *inward* actings of grace, and all instances of outward duties, and that *always* while we live in this world, are required of us hereunto' (John Owen).

From all that has been said it should be evident that the Christian needs to exercise the greatest possible care, *daily*, over the inward purity of his heart, earnestly opposing *the first motions* of every fleshly lust, inordinate affection, evil imagination, and unholy passion. The heart is the real seat of holiness. Heart-holiness is the chief part of our conformity to the spiritual law of God, nor is any outward work considered as holy by him if the heart be not right with him – desiring and seeking after obedience to him – for he sees and tries *the heart*. Holiness of heart is absolutely necessary to peace of mind and joy of soul, for only a cleansed heart can commune with the thrice Holy God: 'then keep thy heart *with all diligence*; for out of it are the issues of life' (Prov. 4:23).

In the last paragraph we have said nothing which in anywise clashes with our remarks in the body of this chapter; rather have we emphasized once more another aspect of our subject, namely, the pressing duty which lies upon the Christian to bring his heart and life into fuller conformity with the law. It would be a grievous sin on the part of the writer were he to lower the standard which God has set before us to the level of our present attainments. Vast indeed is the difference between what *we ought to be* and what we actually *are* in our character and conduct, and deep should be our sorrow over this. Nevertheless, if the root of the matter be in us, there will be a longing after, a praying for a pressing forward unto increased personal and practical holiness.

N.B. *This aspect of our theme has been purposely developed by us somewhat disproportionately. The supreme importance of it required fullness of detail. The prevailing ignorance called for a lengthy treatment of the subject. Unless we know what the Rule of Sanctification is, and seek to conform thereto, all our efforts after holiness will and must be wide of the mark. Nothing is more honouring to God, and nothing makes more for our own happiness, than for his law to be revered, loved, and obeyed by us.*

11

Its Instrument

Paul was sent unto the Gentiles 'to open their eyes, to turn them from darkness to light, and from the power of Satan unto God, that they may receive forgiveness of sins and inheritance among them which are *sanctified by faith* that is in me' (Acts 26:18). Two extremes are to be guarded against in connection with the precise relation that faith sustains to the various aspects of salvation: disparaging it, and making too much of it. There are those who expressly deny that faith has any actual part or place in the securing of the same. On the other hand, there are some who virtually make a saviour out of faith, ascribing to it what belongs alone to *Christ*. But if we adhere closely to Scripture and observe all that is said thereon (instead of restricting our attention to a few passages), there is no excuse for falling into either error. We shall therefore make a few remarks with the object of refuting each of them.

'But without faith it is impossible to please God' (Heb. 11:6). We are saved by faith (Luke 7:50). We are justified by faith (Rom. 5:1). We live by faith (Gal. 2:20). We stand by faith (2 Cor. 1:24). We walk by faith (2 Cor. 5:7). We obey by faith (Rom. 1:5). Christ dwells in our hearts by faith (Eph. 3:17). We overcame the world by faith (1 John 5:4). The heart is purified by faith (Acts 15:9). All duties, for

THE DOCTRINE OF SANCTIFICATION

their right motive and end, depend upon it. No trials and afflictions can be patiently or profitably borne unless faith be in exercise. Our whole warfare can only be carried on and finished victoriously by faith (1 Tim. 6:12). All the gifts and graces of God are presented in the promises, and they can only be received and enjoyed by us in a way of believing. It is high worship to be strong in faith giving glory to God. In view of all this, we need not be surprised to read that we are '*sanctified* by faith'.

But *in what way* does faith sanctify us? To answer this question properly we must carefully bear in mind the principal aspects of our subject, which have already been considered by us in the previous chapters of this book. First, faith has nothing to do with the Father's setting us apart and blessing us with all spiritual blessings in Christ before the foundation of the world: it is one of the God-dishonouring and creature-exalting errors of Arminianism to affirm that Christians were elected on the ground that God foresaw they would believe. Second, our faith was in no sense a moving cause to Christ's becoming the Surety of his people and working out for them a perfect holiness before God. Third, faith has no influence in causing the Holy Spirit to separate the elect from the reprobate, for at the moment he does this they are dead in trespasses and sins, and therefore totally incapable of performing any spiritual acts. Fourth, faith will not contribute anything unto the Christian's glorification, for *that* is solely the work of God; the subject of it being entirely passive therein. 'Whom he justified, them he also glorified.'

Thus faith, important though it be, plays only a secondary and subordinate part in sanctification. It is neither the originating, the meritorious, nor the efficient cause of it, but only the *instrumental*. Yet faith *is necessary* in order to a saving union with Christ, and until that be effected none of the blessings and benefits which are in him can be received

y us. It seems strange that any who are well versed in the
scriptures and who profess to be subject to their teachings,
should question what has just been affirmed. Take such a
declaration as 'them that believe *to* the saving of the soul'
(Heb. 10:39). True, we are not saved *for* our believing, yet
equally true is it that there is no salvation for any sinner
without his believing. Every blessing we receive from Christ
is in consequence of our being united to him, and therefore
we cannot receive the holiness there is in him until we are
sanctified by faith'. Furthermore, faith is necessary in order
to the reception of the purifying Truth, in order to practical
deliverance from the power of sin, and in order to progress
r growth in personal holiness.

Before proceeding further let it be pointed out that the faith
which the gospel requires, the faith which savingly unites a
sinner to Christ, the faith which issues in sanctification, is
very much more than the bare assent of the mind to what
is recorded in the Scriptures concerning the Lord Jesus; it is
something far different from the mere adoption of certain
evangelical opinions regarding the way of salvation. The
Day to come will reveal the solemn fact that thousands
went down to hell with their heads filled with orthodox
beliefs – which many of them contended for earnestly and
propagated zealously, just as the Mohammedan does with
the tenets and principles of *his* religion. Saving faith, my
reader, is the soul's surrender to and reliance upon the Lord
Jesus Christ as a living, loving, all-sufficient Saviour, and
that, upon the alone but sure testimony of God himself.
When we say 'an all-sufficient Saviour' we mean One
in whom there is a spotless holiness as well as perfect
righteousness for those who come to him.

Faith lays hold of Christ as he is offered to sinners in the
gospel, and he is there presented not only for justification
but also for the sanctification of all who truly believe on
him. The glorious gospel of grace not only heralds One

who delivers from the wrath to come but as giving title t
approach now unto the thrice holy God. Moreover, fait
accepts a *whole* Christ: not only as Priest to atone for u:
but as a King to reign over us. Faith, then, is *the instrumen*
of our sanctification. Faith is the eye which perceives th
gracious provisions which God has made for his people
Faith is the hand which appropriates those provision:
Faith is the mouth which receives all the good that God ha
stored up for us in Christ. Without faith it is impossible t
please God, and without the *exercise* of faith it is impossibl
to make any real progress in the spiritual life.

Many of the Lord's people rob themselves of much o
their peace and joy by confounding faith with its fruit:
they fail to distinguish between the Word of God believe
and what follows from believing it aright. Fruit grows o
the tree, and the tree must exist before there can be frui
True obedience, acceptable worship, growth in grace
assurance of salvation, are what faith produces, and no
what faith itself *is*: they are the effects of faith working, an
not definitions of the nature of faith. Faith derives its bein
from the Word of God, and all its fruits are the result o
believing. What God has spoken in his Word demands belie
from all to whom the Word comes. Faith and the Word o
God, then, are related as the effect and the cause, becaus
'faith cometh by hearing, and hearing by the Word of God
(Rom. 10:17). When faith comes by the *inward* 'hearing'
then we assent to what God has said, and we rely upon hi:
faithfulness to make good what he has promised; until *tha*
has been effected there can be no fruits of faith.

It is, then, of much importance to correctly define wha
faith is, for a mistake at this point is not only dishonourin;
to God, but injurious to the soul and inimical to its peace
Faith is a childlike taking God at his Word and resting or
what he has said. It is a depending on Christ to bestow
those blessings and graces which he has promised to thos

who believe. How is a sin-defiled soul to become a partaker of the cleansing efficacy of the blood of the Lamb? Only by *faith*. The purifying virtue of Christ's blood, and the administration of the Spirit, for the application to make it effectual unto our souls and consciences, is exhibited in the promises of the gospel; and the only way to be made partaker of the good things presented in the promises is by faith. God himself ordained this instrumental efficacy unto faith in the Everlasting Covenant, and nothing is more honouring to him than the exercise of real faith.

Returning to our earlier question, In what way does faith sanctify us? We answer, first, *by uniting us to Christ*, the Holy One. Oneness with Christ is the foundation of all the blessings of the Christian, but it is not until he is actually united to Christ by faith that those blessings are really made over to him. Then it is that Christ is 'made unto us wisdom, and righteousness, and sanctification, and redemption' (1 Cor. 1:30). It is faith which receives Christ's atonement, for God hath set forth Christ 'a propitiation *through faith* in his blood' (Rom. 3:25), and his infinitely meritorious blood not only justifies but sanctifies too. Thus there is no intrinsic virtue in faith itself, instead, its value lies wholly in its being the hand which lays hold of him who possesses infinite virtue. For this very reason faith excludes all boasting (Rom. 3:27), and therefore any 'believing' which produces self-gratulation or results in self-satisfaction is most certainly not the faith of the gospel.

Second, faith sanctifies the believer by enabling him *to enjoy now* what is his in Christ and what will be his in himself in heaven. Faith sets to its seal that the testimony of God is true when he declares that 'we *are* sanctified through the offering of the body of Jesus Christ once for all' (Heb. 10:10). Faith assures its possessor that though he is still a fallen creature in himself, and as such a sinner to the end of his earthly course, yet in Christ he is perfectly holy, having the same immaculate standing before God as does his Head and Surety; for 'as *he* is, so are *we* in this world' (1 John 4:17). Thus faith is 'the evidence of things *not seen*' (Heb. 11:1) by the natural eye, nor felt by the natural senses. Faith projects us out of this scene entirely and carries the heart into heaven itself – not a natural faith, not a preacher-produced faith, but gospel faith, imparted by the Holy Spirit.

But let us not be mistaken at this point. The faith of which we are here treating is not a blind fanaticism. It does not ignore the presence of indwelling sin. It does not close its eyes to the constant activities of the flesh. It refuses to tone down the vile fruits which the flesh produces, by terming them peccadillos, ignorance, mistakes, etc. No, faith has clear vision and perceives the infinite enormity of all that is opposed to God. Faith is honest and scorns the hypocrisy of calling darkness light. But faith not only sees the total depravity of natural self and the horrible filth which fouls every part of it, but it also views the precious blood which has satisfied every claim of God upon those for whom it was shed, and which cleanses from all sin those who put their trust in it. It is neither fanaticism nor presumption for faith to receive at its face value what God has declared concerning the sufficiency of Christ's sacrifice.

Third, faith sanctifies as it *derives grace from* the fullness which there is in Christ. God has constituted the Mediator the Source of all spiritual influences and faith is the instrument by which they are derived from him. Christ is not only a Head of authority to his Church, but also a Head of influence. 'But speaking the truth in love, *may grow up into him* in all things, which is the Head, even Christ: from whom the whole body fitly joined together and compacted by that which every joint supplieth, according to the effectual working in the measure of every part, *maketh increase* of the body unto the edifying of itself in love' (Eph. 4:15, 16). That 'effectual working in the measure of every part' is by supplies of grace being received from Christ, and that grace flows through the appointed channel *of faith*. As the Lord Jesus declared unto the father of the demon-tormented son, 'If thou canst believe, all things are possible to him that believeth' (Mark 9:23); and to the two blind beggars who cried unto him for mercy, 'According to your faith be it unto you' (Matt. 9:29). How earnest and importunate should we be, in begging the Lord to graciously strengthen and increase our faith.

It is by faith laying hold upon a full Christ that the empty soul is replenished. All that we need for time as well as eternity is to be found in him; but the hand of faith must be extended, even though it grasp but the hem of his garment, if virtue is to flow forth from him into us. As Samson's strength was in his locks, so the Christian's strength is in his Head. This the devil knows full well, and therefore does he labour so hard to keep us from Christ, causing the clouds of unbelief to hide from our view the radiant face of the Sun of righteousness, and getting us so occupied with our miserable selves that we forget the great Physician. As it is by the sap derived from the root which makes the branches fruitful, so it is by the virtue which faith draws from Christ that the believer is made to abound in holiness. Hence the exhortation, 'Thou therefore, my son, be strong in the grace that is in Christ Jesus' (2 Tim. 2:1).

Fourth, faith sanctifies because *it cleanses the soul*. 'And God, which knoweth the hearts, bare them witness, giving them the Holy Spirit, even as he did unto us; and put no difference between us and them, *purifying* their hearts by faith' (Acts 15:8, 9). It is by faith the heart is 'sprinkled from an evil conscience' by the blood of Christ. It is by faith the affections are lifted unto things above, and thereby disentangled from the defiling objects of the world. It is by the exercise of faith that the 'inward parts' (Ps. 51:6) are conformed in some measure unto the Rule of righteousness

THE DOCTRINE OF SANCTIFICATION

and holiness, for 'faith worketh by love' (Gal. 5:6), and 'love is the fulfilling of the law' (Rom. 13:10). It is to be duly noted that in Acts 15:9 the apostle did not say 'their hearts *were* purified by faith'; instead, he used the present tense 'purifying', for it is a *continuous process* which lasts as long as the believer is here upon earth. This aspect of our sanctification is not complete till we are released from this world.

Fifth, faith sanctifies because it is by this we *hold communion with Christ*, and communion with him cannot but nourish the principle of holiness within the regenerate. Thus faith is sanctifying in its own nature, for it is exercised upon spiritual objects. 'But we all, with open face beholding (by faith) as in a glass the glory of the Lord, *are changed* into the same image from glory to glory, by the Spirit of the Lord' (2 Cor. 3:18). Faith is a transforming grace because it causes the soul to cleave unto the divine Transformer. As it was faith which made us to first lay hold of Christ, so it impels us to *continue* coming unto him; and if the woman who touched the hem of his garment by faith secured the healing of her body, shall not those who cleave to Christ continue obtaining from him the healing of their spiritual maladies!

Sixth, faith sanctifies because it *appropriates the commandments* of God and produces obedience. We are sanctified 'by the Truth' (John 17:17), yet the Word works not without an act on *our* part as well as of God's. It is naught but blind enthusiasm which supposes that the Scriptures work in us like some magical charm. How solemn is that passage 'but the Word preached did not profit them, not being mixed with faith in them that heard it' (Heb. 4:2). The Word avails us nothing if it be not received into a trustful heart and faith be acted upon it. Therefore do we read, 'seeing ye have purified your souls *in obeying* the truth through the Spirit' (1 Pet. 1:22): it is only as the Truth is received upon the authority of God, given a place in our affections, and yielded to by the will, that our souls are 'purified' by it. The more faith causes us to run in the way of God's commandments, the more is the soul delivered from the defiling effects of self-pleasing.

Seventh, faith sanctifies because it *responds to the various motives* which God has proposed to his people, motives to stir them up unto their utmost endeavours and diligence in using those ways and means which he has appointed for preventing the defilement of sin, and for cleansing the conscience when defilement has been contracted. As faith receives the Word *as God's*, its divine authority awes the soul, subdues enmity, and produces submission. The effects of faith are that the soul trembles at the divine threatenings, yields obedience to the divine precepts, and gladly embraces the divine promises. Herein, and in no other way, do we obtain unfailing evidence of the reality and genuineness of our faith. As the species of a tree is identified by the nature of the fruit which it bears, so the kind of faith we have may be ascertained by the character of the effects which it produces. Some of those effects we have sought to describe in the last few paragraphs.

Its Instrument (Completed)

Having presented an outline in our last chapter of the part which *faith* plays in sanctification, we shall now endeavour, under God, to offer consolation unto some of our sin-burdened, doubt-harassed, Satan-tormented brethren and sisters in Christ. 'Comfort ye, comfort ye *my people*, saith your God' (Isa. 40:1). And why? Because God's children are *the most deeply distressed* people on the face of the earth! Though at times they experience a peace which passeth all understanding, revel in that love which passeth knowledge, and rejoice with joy unspeakable, yet for the most part their souls are much cast down, and fears, bondage, groans, constitute a large part of their experience. They may for a brief season be regaled by the wells and palm trees of Elim, but most of their lives are lived in the 'great howling wilderness' (Deut. 32:10), so that they are often constrained to say, 'Oh that I had wings like a dove for then would I fly away, and be at rest.'

Such a distressful experience causes many of the regenerate to very seriously doubt whether they are real Christians. They cannot harmonize their gloom with the light-heartedness they behold in religious professors all around them. No, and they need not wish to. The superficial and apostate religion of our day is producing nothing but a generation of flighty and frothy characters, who scorn anything sober, serious, and solemn, and who sneer at that which searches, strips, and abases into the dust. God's Isaacs must not expect to be understood and still less appreciated by the 'mocking' Ishmaels (Gen. 21:9), for though these dwell for a while in Abraham's household, yet a different mother has borne them. Unless the sun-distressed and fear-tormented believer is 'as a sparrow alone upon the housetop' (Ps. 102:7), then he will have to say 'mine heritage is unto me as a speckled bird, the birds round about are *against* me' (Jer. 12:9) – there is no oneness, no fellowship.

Many of God's dear children are like Asaph: 'But as for me, my feet were almost gone; my steps had well nigh slipped. For I was envious at the foolish, when I saw the prosperity of the wicked. For there are no bands in their death: but their strength is firm. They are not troubled as other men, neither are they plagued like other men. Therefore pride compasseth them about as a chain: violence covereth them as a garment. Their eyes stand out with fatness: they have more than heart could wish. They are corrupt, and speak wickedly: concerning oppression, they speak loftily' (Ps. 73:2-8). As Asaph beheld the prosperity of these people he was staggered, supposing that God was with *them* and had deserted him.

The spiritual counterpart of this is found in modern Laodicea. There is a generation of professing Christians who appear to enjoy great religious 'prosperity'. They have considerable knowledge of the letter of Scripture; they are experts in 'rightly dividing the Word'; they have great light upon the mysteries of prophecy; and are most successful as 'soul winners'. They have no ups and downs in their experience, no painful twistings and turnings, but go on in a straight course with light hearts and beaming countenances. Providence smiles upon them, and they never have a doubt as to their acceptance in Christ. Satan does not trouble them, nor is indwelling sin a daily plague to them. And the poor Christian, conscious of his weakness, his ignorance, his poverty, his vileness, is sorely tempted to be 'envious' of them, for they seem to have 'more than heart could wish', while the longings of his heart are denied him, and that which he pursues so eagerly continues to elude his grasp.

Ah, but note well some of the other characteristics of this 'prosperous' company. '*Pride* compasseth them about as a chain' (Ps. 73:6). Yes, they are utter strangers to humility and lowliness. They are pleased with their peacock feathers, knowing not that God views the same as 'filthy rags'. Concerning oppression, they speak loftily' (Ps. 73:8). God's children *are* oppressed, sorely oppressed, by their corruptions, by their innumerable failure, by the hidings of the Lord's face, by the accusations of Satan. They are oppressed over the workings of unbelief, over the coldness of their hearts, over the insincerity of their prayers, over their vain imaginations. But these Laodiceans, 'speak loftily', ridiculing such things, and prate of *their* peace, joy and victory. 'Therefore his people, return hither: and waters of a full cup are wrung out to them' (Ps. 73:10), for as *real* Christians listen to the 'testimonies' of the 'higher life' people, they conclude that it would be the height of presumption to regard themselves as Christians at all.

'Behold, these are the ungodly,' continues Asaph, 'who prosper in the (religious) world; they increase in riches (Ps. 73:12). And as he was occupied with them, contrasting his own sad lot, a spirit of discontent and petulance took possession of him. 'Verily I have cleansed my heart in vain' (Ps. 73:13) – what is all my past diligence and efforts worth? I am not 'prosperous' like these professors: I do not have their graces or attainments, I do not enjoy the peace, assurance and victory *they* have. Far from it: 'For all the day long I have been plagued, and chastened every morning' (Ps. 73:14). Ah, *that* was holy Asaph's experience, my reader; is it yours? If so, you are in goodly company, much as the present-day Pharisees may despise you.

Then the Psalmist was checked, and realized his wrong in giving way to such wicked sentiments. 'If I say, I will speak thus behold, I should offend against the generation of thy children' (Ps. 73:15). Yes, the generation of God's children *will be* offended when they hear one of their brethren saying it is 'vain' to use the appointed means of grace because those have not issued in deliverance from indwelling sin. 'When I thought to know this, it was too painful for me; until I went into the sanctuary of God: then understood I *their end*. Surely thou didst set them in slippery places: thou castedst them down into destruction' (Ps. 73:16-18). How unspeakably solemn! Instead of these prosperous Laodiceans having a spiritual experience high above those whose hearts plague them 'all the day long', they were total strangers to real spirituality. Instead of being among the chief favourites of God, they had been set by him in the 'slippery places' of error and false religion, to be eventually 'cast down into destruction'.

What a warning is this, my sin-harassed brother, *not to envy* those who are strangers to the plague of their own hearts, who groan not 'being burdened' (2 Cor. 5:4). and who cry not 'O wretched man that I am' (Rom. 7:24). Envy not the proud Laodiceans, who are 'rich and increased with goods and have need of nothing'; and know not that they are 'wretched, and miserable, and poor, and blind, and naked' (Rev. 3:17). Instead, be thankful if God has made you *poor in spirit* – feeling that you are *destitute* of every spiritual grace and fruit; and to 'mourn' over your barrenness and waywardness; for none other than Christ pronounces such characters 'blessed'. And why should you think it strange if you are among that little company who are *the most distressed people* on earth? Have you not been called into fellowship with Christ, and was *he* not 'The Man of sorrows' while he tabernacled in this world? If he sorrowed and suffered so much in enduring the penalty of sin, will you complain because God is now making you groan daily under the felt workings of the power of sin?

The fact of the matter is that very much of that which now passes for sanctification is nothing but a species of pharisaism, which causes its deluded votaries to thank God that they are not like other men; and sad it is to find many of the Lord's people adding to their miseries by grieving over how far *they* come behind the lofty attainments which they imagine these boasters have reached unto. A true and God-honouring 'Christian testimony', my reader, does not consist in magnifying *self*, by telling of attainments and excellencies which, with apparent humility, are ascribed to divine enabling. No indeed, very far from it. That 'witness' which is most honouring to the Lord is one which acknowledges his amazing grace and which magnifies his infinite patience in continuing to bear with such an ungrateful, hard-hearted, and unresponsive wretch.

The great mistake made by most of the Lord's people is in hoping to discover *in themselves* that which is to be found in Christ alone. It is this, which causes them to become so envious and discontented when they behold the spurious holiness of some and the carnal attractiveness of others. There is such a thing as 'the goodliness' of the flesh, which is 'as the flower of the field' (Isa. 40:6), yet as the very next verse tells us 'the Spirit of the LORD bloweth upon it'. But so easily are the simple deceived today they often mistake such 'goodliness' for godliness. Why, my reader, a man (or woman) in his personal makeup may be as meek and tractable as a lamb, he may be constitutionally as kind and grateful as a spaniel, and he may be temperamentally as cheerful as a lark; yet there is not a grain of *grace* in these natural qualities. On the other hand, the Christian, in his natural temperament, is likely to be as gloomy as an owl or as wild as a tiger; yet that does not disprove grace within him.

> 'For ye see your calling, brethren, how that not many wise men after the flesh, not many mighty, not many noble, are called: But God hath chosen the *foolish* things of the world to confound the wise; and God hath chosen the *weak* things of the world to confound the things which are mighty; and *base* things of the world, and things which are *despised,* hath God chosen, yea and things which are not (non-entities, *ciphers*) to bring to nought things that are: that no flesh should glory in his presence' (1 Cor. 1:26-29).

If this passage were *really* received at its face value, many of God's sin-afflicted and doubting children would find the key that unlocks much which is bewildering and grievous in their experience.

In his determination to magnify his sovereign grace God has selected many of *the very worst* of Adam's fallen race to be the everlasting monuments of his fathomless mercy – those whom Luther was wont to designate 'The devil's riff-raffs'. This is very evident too from 'Go out quickly into the streets and lanes of the city, and bring in hither the *poor*, and the *maimed*, and the *halt*, and the *blind*' (Luke 14:21) the most *unlikely* ones as guests for a royal feast, the waifs and strays of society! There are thousands of moral, upright, amiable people who are never effectually called by the Spirit; whereas moral perverts, thieves, and awful-tempered ones are regenerated. When such are born again they still have vile inclinations, horrible dispositions, fiery tempers, which are very hard to control, and are subject to temptations that many of the unregenerate have no first-hand acquaintance with.

Hundreds more of God's children, whose animal spirits are much quieter by nature and whose temperament is more even and placid, yet are plagued by a spirit of pride and self-righteousness, which is just as hateful in the sight of God as moral degeneracy is to respectable worldlings. Now unless the thoughts of such are formed from the Scriptures, they are sure to entertain erroneous conceptions which will destroy their peace and fill them with doubts and fears, for upon a fuller discovery and clearer sight of the sea of corruption within, they will conclude they have never passed from death unto life. But to call into question our regeneration because we fail to obtain deliverance from the power of indwelling sin, is a great mistake; the new birth neither removes nor refines the flesh, but is the reception of a nature that feels sin to be an intolerable burden, and that yearns after holiness above everything else.

If I have really come to Christ as a leprous and bankrupt sinner, utterly despairing of self-help, and have put my trust in the sufficiency of his sacrifice, the Scripture affirms that God has made Christ to be *sanctification to me* (1 Cor. 1:30) and that I have received a spirit of holiness from him. Now *faith* accepts this blessed fact notwithstanding an ocean of corruption and the continued raging of sin within. My peace of mind will, then, very largely depend upon *faith's continued apprehension* of the perfect salvation which God has provided for his people in Christ, and which in heaven they shall enjoy in their own persons. After the sinner has come to Christ savingly, the Holy Spirit gives him a much fuller discovery of his vileness, and makes him a hundredfold more conscious of how much there is in his heart that is opposed to God than ever he realized previously; and unless *faith* be daily in exercise, the activities of the flesh will slay his assurance – instead, they ought to drive him closer and closer to Christ.

O my Christian reader, what a difference it would make were you to steadily realize the truth that, every temptation you encounter, every defeat you suffer, every distressing experience you pass through, is a call and a challenge for the exercise of *faith*. You complain that you are still the subject of sin, that it cleaves to you as the flesh does to your bones, that it mixes with your duties and defiles every act you perform. You often feel that you are nothing but sin. When you attempt to walk with God, inward evil rises up and stops you. When you read his Word or endeavour to pray, unbelieving thoughts, carnal imaginations, worldly lusts, seek to possess your soul. You strive against them; but in vain. Instead of improvement, things grow worse. You beg of God for humility, and pride rises higher; you cry to him for more patience, but apparently his ear is closed. Ah, you are now learning the painful truth that in your flesh there dwelleth '*no* good thing'.

Yes, but what is a poor soul to do in such a harrowing case? How is it possible for him to preserve *any* peace in his conscience? When the believer is so sorely attacked by sin and Satan, how is he to defend himself? Nothing but *faith* in the sure Word of God can keep him from sinking into abject despair. This is the very time for him to maintain his trust in the sufficiency of Christ's blood and the excellency of his imputed righteousness. His faith is now being tried by the fire that it may come forth as gold. It is by such experiences *the genuineness* of his faith is put to the proof. The believer cast into the furnace that faith may conflict with unbelief, and though he will be hard put to it, yet victory is sure. The proof of his victory is faith's perseverance (amid a thousand waverings) unto the end. Remember, my reader, that the test of perseverance is not how we act in the face of success, but how we conduct ourselves under a long series of defeats. 'For a just man falleth seven times, and *riseth up again*' (Prov. 24:16).

Let it not be overlooked that we can no more take our place before God now as accepted worshippers without a perfect holiness, than we can enter heaven without it; but that perfect holiness is to be found *in Christ alone* - the practical holiness of the Christian is, at present, but a very, very faint reflection of it. The more I feel my utter unworthiness and total unfitness to approach unto God and call upon him in my *own* name, the more thankful I should be for the Mediator, and the unspeakable privilege of calling upon God in *Christ's* name. And it is faith which counts upon the glorious fact that the thrice holy God *can* exercise his grace and goodness toward one so vile as I, and that, consistently with his majesty and justice – Christ has honoured the law infinitely more than my sins dishonour it. One who feels that, as a Christian, he is 'an utter failure', and who is conscious of his continued abuse of God's mercies, can only draw nigh to God with confidence as he *exercises* faith in the infinite merits of Christ.

As we stated at the beginning, our principal object in writing this chapter is, under God, to comfort his sin-distressed, doubt-harassed, Satan-tormented people. We are not unmindful that among the ranks of nominal Christians there are, on the one hand, many 'having a form of godliness, but denying the power thereof: ...ever learning and never able to come to the knowledge of the Truth' (2 Tim. 3:5, 7), who will regard as highly 'dangerous' much of what we have said; while on the other hand, there are 'ungodly men, turning the grace of our God into lasciviousness (Jude 4), who are likely to abuse the same by adopting it as an intellectual opinion, from which they may derive peace in their defiance of God. Yet notwithstanding these likely eventualities, we shall not withhold a needful portion of the children's bread.

Those who claim to have received the 'second blessing' and be 'entirely sanctified' in themselves, have never seen their hearts in the light of God. Those who boast of their sinless perfection are deceived by Satan, and 'the truth is not in them' (1 John 1:8). Two things ever go together in the experience of a genuine believer: a growing discovery of the vileness of self, and a deepening appreciation of the preciousness of Christ. There is no solid ground for a believer to rest upon till he sees that Christ has *fully* answered to God for him. In exact proportion to his *faith* will be his peace and joy. 'Ye are *complete* in him' (Col. 2:10): believers now possess a perfect holiness in the Covenant Head, but at present they are far from being perfect in the grace which flows to them from him. God honours and rewards that faith which is exercised upon our holiness in Christ: not necessarily by subduing sin or granting victory over it, but by enabling its possessor to continue cleaving to Christ as his only hope.

O my Christian reader, be content to be nothing in yourself, that *Christ* may be your *all*. O to truly say, 'He must increase, but I must decrease' (John 3:30). Growth in grace is a being brought more and more off from self-complacency and self-dependency, to an entire reliance upon Christ and the free grace of God through him. This temper is begun in the believer at regeneration, and like the tiny mustard seed it at last develops into a large tree. As the Christian grows in grace he finds himself to be increasingly full of wants, and further off than ever from being worthy to receive the supply of them. More and more the spirit of a beggar possesses him. As the Spirit grants more light, he has a growing realization of the beauty of holiness, of what Christ is entitled to from him; and there is a corresponding self-loathing and grief because he is so unholy in himself and fails so miserably to render unto Christ his due.

Fellowship with God and walking in the light as he is in the light, so far from filling the Christian with self-satisfaction, causes him to groan because of his darkness and filthiness – the clearer light now making manifest what before was unperceived. Nothing is more perilous to the soul than that we should be occupied with *our* achievements, victories, enjoyments. If Paul was in danger of being exalted by the abundance of the revelations vouchsafed him, can the danger be less of *our* being puffed up with thoughts of spiritual progress, spiritual conquests, spiritual excellencies. And yet the cherishing of *such* thoughts is the very thing which is now being increasingly encouraged by the religious quacks of the day. No matter what fellowship with Christ be enjoyed, what growth in grace be made, it will ever remain true that 'we that are in this tabernacle do groan, being burdened' (2 Cor. 5:4).

So far from what we have said in this chapter encouraging a real Christian to entertain low views of sin, it is only in the vital and experimental knowledge of the same that a life of holiness begins. Nothing will cause a renewed soul to hate sin so much as a realization of God's *grace*; nothing will move him to mourn so genuinely over his sins as a sense of Christ's dying love. It is *that which breaks his heart*: the realization that there is so much in him that is opposed to Christ. But a life of holiness is a life of faith (the heart turning daily to Christ), and the fruits of faith are genuine repentance, true humility, praising God for his infinite patience and mercy, pantings after conformity to Christ, praying to be made more obedient, and continually confessing our disobedience. Day-dreaming about complete deliverance

217

from indwelling sin, seeking to persuade ourselves that the flesh is becoming less active, cannot counter-balance the humbling reality of our present state; but our corruptions should not quench a true gospel hope.

Those who have read the previous chapters of this book cannot suppose that we have any design to lower the standard of the Christian life, or to speak peace to deluded souls who 'profess that they know God; but in works deny Him' (Titus 1:16). Some indeed may charge us with encouraging light views of the sinfulness of sin, yet it must be remembered that the grand truth of divine *grace* has ever appeared 'dangerous' to mere human wisdom. A worldly moralist must think it subservient of the very foundations of virtue to proclaim to men, *without regard* to what they have done, and *without stipulation* as to what they are to do, 'Believe on the Lord Jesus Christ and thou shalt be saved' If I believed that says the unrenewed man, I would take my fill of sin, without fear or remorse. Ah, but a saving faith from God is always accomplished by a principle which hates sin and loves holiness; and the greatest grief of its possessor is, that its aspirations are so often thwarted. But those very thwartings are the testings of faith, and should daily drive us back to Christ for fresh cleansings. Lord, increase our faith.

Other Books of Interest

in the

Christian Heritage Imprint

LIFE OF FAITH

WHAT HAS GOD DONE FOR YOU?

A.W. PINK

The Life of Faith

What has God done for you?

A. W. Pink

f your spiritual life seems to be going nowhere – A.W. Pink can help.

This is no superficial '10 steps guide' that skims above the surface of thought and satisfaction. This is a popular look at deep subjects that will promote real change in your life.

In it you will find answers on the foundational subjects of atonement, salvation, the Law and spiritual growth as well as help in the practical areas of temptation, testing and backsliding.

A.W. Pink (1886 – 1952) was born in England and converted in his mid 20's. After just two months of his studies at Moody Bible College in Chicago he was called to a pastorate in Colorado. He was engaged as a pastor until 1921 after which he decided to concentrate on writing and speaking at conferences. The next year he started a monthly magazine *'Studies in the Scriptures'*, which he edited until his death in 1952.

Most of Pink's published works are collections from these magazine articles. This title gathers together lightly edited articles, with selections from his other published works, about how to live in Christ.

The result is a balanced guide on how God helps you achieve the improvement in your Christian life that he wants.

ISBN 1-85792-047-3

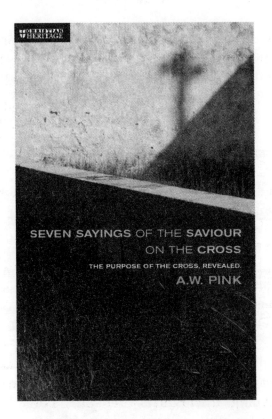

SEVEN SAYINGS OF THE SAVIOUR
ON THE CROSS

THE PURPOSE OF THE CROSS, REVEALED.

A.W. PINK

Seven Sayings of the Saviour on the Cross

The purpose of the cross, revealed

A.W. Pink

Seven of the most famous sayings in the world - more widely recognised now than when they were uttered 2000 years ago – but are they *better known*?

"Father forgive them for they know not what they do"

"I tell you the truth, today you will be with me in paradise."

"Dear woman, here is your son, here is your mother."

"Eli, Eli, lama sabachthani? (My God, my God, why have you forsaken me?)"

"I thirst."

"It is finished."

"Father, into your hands I commit my spirit."

If you want to know what Jesus really meant by these famous sayings then Pink is a reliable guide.

'A classic treatment of Jesus' seven sayings on the cross. Those who know Pink writings will concur that this is Pink at his very best. As only Pink could, he extracts a wealth of devotional material from each saying. Thoroughly recommended to all.'

The Evangelical Presbyterian

ISBN 1-85792-059-7

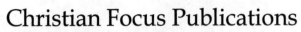

Christian Focus Publications

publishes books for all ages

Our mission statement –

STAYING FAITHFUL

In dependence upon God we seek to help make His infallible Word, the Bible, relevant. Our aim is to ensure that the Lord Jesus Christ is presented as the only hope to obtain forgiveness of sin, live a useful life and look forward to heaven with Him.

REACHING OUT

Christ's last command requires us to reach out to our world with His gospel. We seek to help fulfill that by publishing books that point people towards Jesus and help them develop a Christ-like maturity. We aim to equip all levels of readers for life, work, ministry and mission.

Books in our adult range are published in three imprints.

Christian Focus contains popular works including biographies, commentaries, basic doctrine and Christian living. Our children's books are also published in this imprint.

Mentor focuses on books written at a level suitable for Bible College and seminary students, pastors, and other serious readers. The imprint includes commentaries, doctrinal studies, examination of current issues and church history.

Christian Heritage contains classic writings from the past.

Christian Focus Publications, Ltd
Geanies House, Fearn,
Ross-shire, IV20 1TW, Scotland, United Kingdom
info@christianfocus.com

For details of our titles visit us on our website
www.christianfocus.com